THE UNIVERSITY IMPERATIVE

DELIVERING SOCIO-ECONOMIC BENEFITS FOR OUR WORLD

NICHOLAS MATHIOU

Title: The University Imperative: Delivering Socio-economic Benefits for Our World

Author: Nicholas Mathiou

ISBN: 9780645360424

Strategic Planning | Organisational Development | Social Impact

Book Production: www.bevryanpublish.com

A catalogue record for this book is available from the National Library of Australia

Are you looking to make a positive impact for our world and transform lives for the better?

Are you seeking to deliver great socio-economic benefits from your university?

Are you trying to navigate the effect that dynamic and competitive environments are having on your university's ability to derive impact?

Given our turbulent environments, is your university grappling with choosing what to do to derive impact and how to get that done?

If you answered yes to any of these questions, welcome to a group of dedicated people who know the importance that universities make to our society; people who are striving to make sure great socio-economic benefits are derived from universities now and well into the future.

CONTENTS

DEDICATION

To Natalie, Isabella, and George

ACKNOWLEDGEMENTS

Thanks to Stephen O'Grady for his endless patience, and whose editorial polish helped distil a collection of concepts, words and discussions into the coherent chapters of this book. Any incoherence is due entirely to me! I highly recommend Stephen.

He can be contacted at ogrady.stephen@gmail.com.

'What was happening could be described as a great ship being turned and blunted and shoved about and pulled around by many small tugs. Once turned by tide and tugs, it must set a new course and start its engines turning. On the bridge, which is the planning centre, the question must be asked: All right, I know now where I want to go. How do I get there, and where are the lurking rocks and what will the weather be?'

—John Steinbeck, 'The Winter of Our Discontent'

Ever since their establishment as institutions of higher education and research, universities have been different. Their evolution across the past ten centuries has seen them infused with an enduring ethos: to benefit society. Irrespective of individual institutional personalities and the manifold geographical coordinates of universities in general, this ethos remains a distinguishing characteristic of any such institute of higher learning. A university is still a community of teachers and scholars, and therefore remains a veritable epicentre of ideas, a concept factory, the rightful birthplace of innovations and products that make the world a better place in which to live; it is a think tank for the betterment of society, an environment where the very practice of education is an exercise in social enrichment.

Certainly, that remains the intent. However, today we live in a world of constant change, uncertainty and unprecedented challenges, a social situation accentuated by the global events of 2020 and 2021. We find ourselves in profoundly difficult territory.

On the face of it, universities continue to operate according to their broad traditional ethos; however, they are increasingly required to question whether they have the societal cut-through expected of institutions of higher education and research. Are the graduates emerging from universities today scholars in the truest sense of the word? Are they the thought leaders and change managers who are capable of not just meeting the demands of an uncertain environment but also transforming it for the greater good? Are the products at the end of the university assembly line utilised in the delivery of social benefit?

Achieving that cut-through and hitting those societal targets no longer happens as a matter of course; the digital revolution has seen to this. Technologies have changed the ways we think and interact forever, not least in terms of information and know-how, and how these are acquired and shared.

A new currency is at play in the business of knowledge, and the modern values of higher education and research have come under pressure. The academic foundations and research rigour that once positioned universities on a higher plane are now under siege from easily accessed information (frequently camouflaged as expert knowledge). Multinational tech companies have provided global platforms for the convenient proliferation of opinion in the absence of verified facts which run counter to universities' endeavours and ethos.

What of society-serving universities and the platforms they provide for scholars and researchers, and the products of their academic enterprise? This prescient question has risen ominously as the university-funding model has been depleted and dented and ultimately damaged by a turbulent economic landscape, competition, the loss of traditional market share, and the ever-tightening public funding available to support university activities.

The need for universities to play their more than noble part in addressing societal issues has never been so clear. The onset of the global pandemic and its implications for health and governance into the future has amplified this need. Unless the role of the university is reinvigorated in proficient fashion, further challenges of profound import lay waiting for the people of this planet. There can be no doubt that universities—institutions of higher education and research, with their communities of teachers and scholars—are the entities best placed to meet these challenges.

Society needs universities to stay relevant and provide benefits for all their stakeholders, but staying relevant in a world of change *requires* change. And while a new or renewed way forward must be forged, it is incumbent on any university not only to do the right thing but also do it in the right way.

Staying relevant requires intent, focus, proficiencies and organisational character. It means shaking off moribund shackles of intellectual isolation, and re-engineering university mechanisms to harness the knowledge and energies of educators and researchers determined to flourish in the face of exponential change and challenges.

At the same time, the benefits of the educators' and researchers' work must accrue to the largest social cohort. If this does not happen, universities will not achieve their mission and their relevance will wane. Educators and researchers must be provided with the necessary platforms to nurture their sense of opportunity, allowing them to reach beyond campus boundaries and seek out tangible collaborations that can optimise the impact of their work on a broad and meaningful scale.

The aim of *The University Imperative* is to present universities of all shapes and sizes around the world with a sense of what is required in this current climate. It constructs a framework with which universities can confidently calibrate their operations. The enduring goal of the university has not changed; delivering a beneficial impact for society remains the order of the day. What *has* changed is the emergent need for commercial rigour in the delivery of social benefits.

Across nine chapters, *The University Imperative* constructs a conceptual scaffold that considers the bearing of universities in this hectic social space while also keeping a measured eye on the resources at their disposal. Any inclination to plot a way forward using rankings and recruitment as though they were GPS coordinates must be resisted. Rather, the abiding importance of tertiary education and research must be reasserted, perhaps recalibrated, so universities can deliver the graduate and research outcomes that make our new world of perpetual flux a better place for all.

'We might have the proudest tradition in the League but we haven't won a premiership in nineteen years. Tradition, tradition, tradition. We've been strangled by it. The days when recruits would flock to the Club from all over the country simply because of its name are long since gone. It's no good waiting for players to come to you; you've got to go out there into the marketplace and fight for them.'

—David Williamson, 'The Club'

KEY THEMES

- Changing role of the 21st-century university

- Competitive pressures brought about by technological advances

- Understanding the need to navigate dynamic new environments

- Choosing what to do and how to get it done

The traditional importance of universities to economic and social prosperity is enduring and far-reaching. There is an abundance of documented evidence that confirms the positive impact of university studies and expert knowledge on the wealth of nations and population wellbeing. There is no question that universities have been cornerstones of society. It is therefore almost inconceivable that their place in our world is at risk; however, with their relevance under siege, the future existence of universities will be called into doubt unless they respond to global circumstances.

We live and learn in a changed and changing world. This social space where we once set down roots and went about achieving our dreams and ambitions with some certainty is no longer the same. Everything moves differently now: faster, more furiously, in directions we once thought not possible. Disruption is not destined to become the new normal; it is here already. We all lead disrupted lives today. The changes have been seismic and are all around us. Economies and societies are transforming at an unprecedented pace. Once familiar industries and organisations have a different look, their workforces often unrecognisable from previous times.

In the midst of this economic and social turbulence are our universities, not isolated, and not immune. They face unprecedented challenges brought about by rapidly advancing technologies, shifting demographics, trade liberalisation, and, more recently, the Covid-19 pandemic. Although universities do continue to compete, they do so with reduced student numbers, and are up against private organisations and new service providers entering the knowledge and expertise sector. The harsh business reality is that many universities are now offering products or services that students can obtain more affordably elsewhere while gaining equal or similar benefits.

With the pressure this imposes on universities' funding models, it is tempting for them to respond by offering more non-differentiated programs, more resources and more funding, or by simply increasing efficiency; however, such responses are increasingly unlikely to succeed in the current environment. Regardless of how many programs are offered, or how many publications or research grant applications are lodged, or how many networking events are hosted and promoted, universities will not get ahead of the game without taking a hard look at their organisational direction, and their structures and characters. While most universities have traditionally excelled at what they do, this is no longer sufficient, and universities worldwide need to reconsider how they approach the business of being a university in the 21st century.

This is a problem faced by universities everywhere. It has evolved as technological advances have altered the value placed on knowledge and its delivery in globalised economies. However, while this is definitely a problem, it is one that can be overcome. Universities can turn uncertainty into opportunity by embracing adaptability and innovation, and recasting strategies that lead to a more efficient investment of resources and more productive outcomes.

Universities must reinvigorate their reasons for existence. They must find a way to regain relevance and remain valuable to society. They must find a framework for forward thinking as they move into a future of innovation.

To achieve these important goals, a considered insight into the predicament is necessary. It is important to reflect on the way in which universities have contributed to society, consider the traditional tertiary approaches that have underpinned this contribution, and highlight the changed circumstances and risks universities now face. In this context, the two pillars of university functions that are impacted are (1) learning and knowledge, and (2) research and innovation.

Learning and knowledge: Perhaps the most significant and broadly understood contribution of universities has been equipping students with the knowledge and skills that benefit them as individuals and as contributors to society, thereby enhancing society on a wide scale. Universities have also been traditionally recognised for generating quality knowledge that can be utilised by all in the community to create wealth and improve living standards.

Society continues to need universities to create high-order knowledge to address its needs and issues, but the call for universities to impart knowledge has been eroded by alternative sources online. We now live in a hyper-connected world where cumulative knowledge from across the globe is readily accessible. There is a wealth of important information freely available at our fingertips through high-quality lectures and information sessions on virtually any topic. Universities are no longer the first port of call to access knowledge, which means that considerable pressure is being placed on student enrolments and associated funding models. This in turn reduces the ability of universities to undertake the necessary research to create new knowledge.

Research and innovation: The second pillar of university functions relates to the application of research outcomes beyond academia. This is perhaps a lesser-known contribution that universities have made to society, but the evidence surrounds us. The raw materials used to build today's digital world of computers and the internet have their origins in university-based innovations. Many of the world's most important health breakthroughs and medical devices have emerged from first steps taken in university laboratories. Many programs that attend to the needs of individuals and communities have emerged from, and have been evaluated and improved by, our universities.

It is clear that throughout the course of history individual universities have been essential for innovativeness and improving lives. Today, however, the research function of universities faces intense competition from both inside and outside the sector. The most effective strategies and solutions to societal problems are not necessarily those brought forward by university researchers. Policymakers and potential investors, for example, can and will look elsewhere for innovation and impact.

Crucially, the idea of advancing research outcomes from universities through single-discipline and single-party domains is virtually redundant. Digital platforms are already facilitating significant collaboration, bringing together expertise and resources from every corner of the globe to address problems. Where the scope of university research is focusing, knowledge is expanding exponentially.

In such a challenging environment, there is no doubt that universities need to evolve, but how? We need to unravel the complexities.

Society needs universities to thrive, but in the current climate many face stalling student enrolments, stagnating funding, and reduced balance-sheet capacity. Traditional strategies that have previously held universities in good stead are fast becoming, or are already, obsolete. In response, some universities may be tempted to discard all traditional strategies. This would be a mistake. Some universities may mount a response by trying everything. This, too, would be a mistake.

This raises the difficult question of knowing exactly what the new role of universities in society is, if not the creating and imparting of knowledge. If this knowledge role is to remain paramount, what is the nature or quality of the knowledge universities impart that continues to set them apart from an array of alternative sources of knowledge in society today?

At the core of every university is immense capability. Universities remain integral to delivering great benefits for society; however, they cannot be everything to everyone, and the universities most likely to succeed are those that take notice of consumer expectations, wants and needs, and then position themselves better than their competitors to address these expectations proactively.

How do universities decide what they should do? And when they have decided, how do they implement that decision?

The University Imperative responds to these core questions across the nine forthcoming chapters. In the four chapters in Part I (Organisational Direction), an endeavour is made to press pause—if this can be countenanced—and establish organisational direction for a modern-day university.

In the five chapters in Part II (Organisational Character), a conceptual manual is assembled outlining ways to implement organisational direction and thrive in a new and emerging business landscape.

Chapter 1 commences by identifying the north stars, three constants that universities can revert to in this time of great change.

PART I

ORGANISATIONAL DIRECTION

'Trust yourself, trust the road, trust the weather, and trust your destination! This quarto-trust can create a miraculously successful journey!'

—Mehmet Murat ildan

NORTH STARS

'When winds and waves a mutual contest wage,

These foaming anger, those impelling rage,

Thy blissful light can cheer the dismal gloom,

And foster hopes beyond a wat'ry doom.'

—John William Smith, 'The Lighthouse',
from 'Terrors of Imagination; and Other Poems'

KEY THEMES

- Setting organisational direction requiring cognisance of major shifts in the world

- Adapting universities' pedagogies to the changing nature of global workforces

- Determining the role of universities in developing innovation practices and entrepreneurial mindsets

- Aligning university research with efforts to solve the issues of the world

Meeting the challenges that universities face in the dynamic environment of today commences with determining direction. Clearly, universities need to mobilise their resources in different ways to manage and move forward with confidence, but to what end, and in what direction? How can universities set their bearings to remain relevant to the issues of today?

Examining major trends and demographic shifts, and the associated roles that universities play therein, presents answers and opportunities. A cursory examination of these trends and shifts reveals the changing nature of the workforce, and the sharp rise in entrepreneurship on the back of digital advancement. It also points to a litany of enduring and emerging societal needs.

THREE NORTH STARS

By maintaining an assured focus on each of the three north stars outlined below, universities can successfully navigate our changing times.

1. The changing nature of workforces

Economies, industries and organisations are transforming, driven by trade liberalisation and advancing technologies. This transformation is dramatically affecting the nature of workforces around the world. Many current jobs will no longer be prevalent by 2030, given, among other things, the rise of automation and artificial intelligence. Many new jobs, some yet to be defined or created, will arise because of the technological platforms emerging right now. There is also a massive trend towards work on demand, also known as the 'gig economy'. The enduring impact of the global pandemic on world economies has only accelerated this process.

A globally accessible labour force like none before now exists. Employers and workers can easily connect, transact and collaborate across geographies. Teams of talented and trained professionals are now able to come together seamlessly to work on projects as highly-skilled people pursue multiple careers throughout their working lives.

As a result, the requirements of employers and employees are changing rapidly, and it is beholden on universities to ensure that their offerings to students are evolving as well. Only in this way can universities continually provide students with the additional and updated skill sets required to flourish in our rapidly evolving world.

In this climate of change, the so-called 'soft' skills (e.g. teamwork, client engagement, project management, capacity to learn and synthesise solutions from diverse information sources, negotiation, persuasion, creativity) are an important objective for education and training. Experiential-based learning is therefore required where students are immersed in the acquisition and application of existing and new knowledge to solve problems. The imparting of knowledge, together with the development of the skills and attributes required to navigate the changing natures of workforces, are in great demand.

The ability of universities to meet demand and provide evidence-based pedagogy and experiential-based learning environments is clearly critical. This can be a major differentiating factor for universities and one that alternative providers may find difficult to match.

Maintaining focus on this north star (equipping graduates with the skill sets needed in new workforces) will serve universities well in navigating the choppy waters of change.

2. The rise of innovation and entrepreneurship

The digital revolution has democratised knowledge, empowered consumers, and spawned scores of new organisations. Access to customers and markets, products and services, labour and capital is no longer in the hands of the few but is now available to us all. Major barriers to entrepreneurship have gone and businesses can now reach, quickly and affordably, virtually anyone, anywhere, anytime to deliver anything.

All organisations recognise the need to innovate through new markets, new products and services, and new business models. Larger established organisations, under competitive pressure, are demanding employees capable of creating better businesses within their confines (now labelled 'intrapreneurship', but more commonly known as innovation).

We continue to see a staggering shift towards entrepreneurship over employment, and the accompanying heightened demand for innovation and entrepreneurial skill sets. This means that the acquisition of the knowledge and skills associated with innovation and entrepreneurialism is becoming an important objective for education and training.

Just as universities are charged with keeping a watchful eye on the skills and knowledge demanded by employers and changed workforces, so too must they maintain a focus on the skills required by graduates to be successful and impactful in innovation and entrepreneurship. The combination of knowledge and the development of the skills and attributes required for innovation and entrepreneurialism are in great demand.

It is crucial for universities to use this north star and provide evidence-based pedagogy and experiential-based learning environments to address this major shift.

3. Addressing societal needs

Many of the world's challenges—and they are many—have yet to be resolved. Issues to be addressed range from the sustainable utilisation of resources to mitigate effects on our environment, to the provision of sustainable health services for an ageing population, to ensuring the wellbeing of impoverished people, to countering violence and substance abuse, and so on.[1]

There is now global recognition that multi-disciplinary, multi-party approaches are required to find complex solutions to such major societal issues. Governments alone cannot address these issues, and they are increasingly taking on a collaborative role as designers and commissioners of services to address societal issues. But governments face fiscal constraints, and this is intensified by a combination of high debt levels, depleted revenues, rising unemployment, stalling growth, and increasing demand for public interventions and their related expenditure. An accelerating demand for social and environmental funding is outstripping broader economic growth.

Governments are, therefore, actively seeking sustainable service-provision and funding models. Capital markets are responding, and innovative financial structures to support the broad scale delivery of interventions are emerging. Pay-for-outcomes financial structures, for example, require service providers to carry the risk of delivering a social outcome (although they do reward them for successfully doing so).

In this competitive context, universities continue to have immense capabilities across many different disciplines and evidently have a collaborative role to play here. They can, and do, play an important role in articulating the nature of problems; conceptualising new or improved models; developing policy; crafting appropriate programs and interventions; piloting models, programs and interventions; educating workforces that can address societal needs; and evaluating achievements of desired outcomes.

Universities inform and provide the independent, evidence-based solutions that address and resolve immense challenges to society. By driving new knowledge, university research remains critical to success. It is clear that partnerships are required that facilitate the wide-scale delivery of evidence-based programs, coupled with sustainable outcomes-based funding models. There is a massive call to mobilise resources effectively to address unresolved global challenges.

By maintaining their gaze on this third north star (societal needs), universities can mobilise resources to manage a pathway through the environments of change.

SETTING DIRECTION

Universities can focus on these three north stars regardless of changing environments. By identifying major trends, demographic shifts and societal needs, universities can continue to pinpoint the associated roles that keep them integral to society. These north stars can and must be utilised to set direction, which will be fundamental to success.

Consideration of the following three questions can help universities set their direction:

> Question 1: Whom do we serve?
> Question 2: What is our ambition?
> Question 3: What is our value?

Clearly, universities exist for the betterment of society. Fundamentally and ultimately, they serve the public by identifying and responding to global challenges and significant societal needs. The ambition (and arguably obligation) of universities must be to address these challenges; the value they offer society in doing so is profound. However, setting direction alone, although necessary, is insufficient for success. Universities must also galvanise action toward the achievement of the chosen direction, and establishing a strong sense of purpose throughout the organisations can assist in this regard.

The next step along this conceptual pathway takes us to universities' spheres of impact, and an understanding of how universities materialise benefits for our world.

Chapter 1 Endnotes

1. There are many major global trends that require the attention of universities, governments, industry, private enterprise and not-for-profit organisations. It is beyond the scope of this book to canvass all. However, there are a few points worth noting:

- Populations are ageing as healthcare costs are rising. People aged sixty and over made up 8% of the population of developed nations in 1950, 15% in 2005, and this number is projected to reach 26% by 2050. In most of the developed world, healthcare spending is growing faster than gross domestic product (GDP).
- Within emerging nations, a 'youth bulge' is leading to increased pressure to deliver job-rich and inclusive growth for the next generation.
- Environments and natural resources required to sustain economic prosperity will be ever more stressed as the world population grows from seven to almost ten billion over the next thirty years. Climate change is affecting everyone. Water, food and energy security are impacted. Migration and immigration ensue, and have profound influence on social cohesion, workforces, and economic development. There is a profound need to sustainably utilise resources and manage diminishing resources in the context of growing and shifting populations. A need for sustainability in the face of rising inequality leads to increased demand for government intervention.
- Investment in research and development to provide solutions to these challenges is increasing across the globe. There is recognition that businesses and communities need to shift to more sustainable models. We are witnessing huge shifts of capital toward social-impact investment. Government research-funding models for university-based research have also shifted from basic research to applied research. Government departments' procurement is shifting toward applied research and outsourcing service delivery. New funding models (e.g. social-investment bonds, social-impact investing) are facilitating outcomes-based service provision and the injection of new funding for programs that deliver socio-economic benefits.
- Many regions are making strategic investments in interdisciplinary science precincts associated with universities and public research organisations. For example: Silicon Valley in the US; the high-tech region in Munich and London's tech start-up boom in Europe; Israel in the Middle East; and Asian innovation clusters in Japan, Taiwan and China.
- Industries are seeking innovations to capture opportunities and counter threats. Organisations are actively searching for innovations from outside their organisational confines.

CHAPTER 2

SPHERES OF IMPACT

'A very little key will open a heavy door.'

—Charles Dickens, 'Hunted Down'

KEY THEMES

- Understanding how to engender a strong and clear purpose

- Understanding how socio-economic benefits materialise from universities thereby helping to establish purpose

- Materialisation of impact in a consistent manner regardless of diversity of underpinning disciplines

- Maximising societal impact from academic impact through collaborative impact

Universities must have a strong sense of purpose in order to establish intent and galvanise shared action within the academic fold. But what is the procedure by which such purpose is identified, agreed upon, and used to garner buy-in from all quarters of the university populace? In the case of universities, to appreciate the true meaning of purpose it is necessary to understand how benefits for society are derived from universities. By focusing our attention outside the campus walls in this way, we can start to design a conceptual framework to be known as the 'spheres of impact'. This framework will ultimately facilitate the precise, purposeful type of thinking that is required across campuses. Only then can a realistic sense of purpose be imparted across the organisational structures, stimulating and releasing potential, and yielding new approaches that enhance the ability to derive impact.

HOW IMPACT MATERIALISES

Ensuring that benefits for society materialise from universities (often described as 'impact') can, at first glance, appear incredibly complex, particularly given the diversity of environments and contexts in which tertiary institutions operate. First, we need to go back to basics, leaning on three core and relatively simple propositions.

Proposition 1

The first proposition is: Benefits from universities materialise through (1) the creation, (2) the provision, and (3) the utilisation of education programs and research outcomes.

The creation of education programs and research outcomes (including products and services) is the result of 'academic impact', and when these programs and outcomes are provided to the community for use and implementation, universities generate 'collaborative impact'. Through the effective utilisation and implementation of these programs, products and services in the community, 'societal impact' is derived.

Irrespective of the myriad differences that exist across internal and external environments, impact from universities manifests from academic impact, to collaborative impact, to societal impact; to be recognised collectively as spheres of impact.

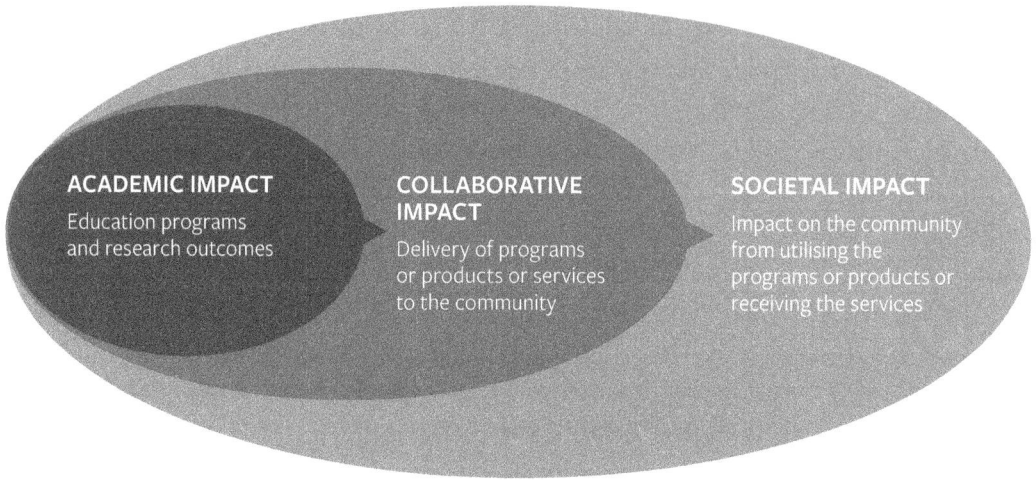

FIGURE 1: SPHERES OF IMPACT

To help demonstrate the spheres-of-impact concept and its range, Table 1 provides examples from such diverse fields as education, life sciences, social sciences, environmental sciences, physical sciences, and the arts. The examples illustrate that regardless of the diversity of underpinning disciplines, impact materialises in a consistent manner.

ACADEMIC IMPACT	COLLABORATIVE IMPACT	SOCIETAL IMPACT
• an education program to improve numeracy in school children	• the number of schools implementing the program	• improved numeracy skills, school outcomes, increased productivity of graduates
• a vaccine candidate	• number of vaccinations	• reduced incidents and related health costs, improved quality of life, increased productivity
• a violence prevention program	• delivery by therapists to people in need	• reduced recidivism, lower public-system costs, improved productivity, and improved wellbeing and quality-of-life
• river catchment plans and schemes to optimise land restoration, management and use	• catchment riverbank and wetland restoration, vegetation of hill slopes, changes to on-farm management and hard engineering	• water security, reduced water costs, reduced sediment dredging and disposal costs, lower flood remedial costs, enhanced tourism from pristine waterways
• an energy efficient and recyclable electrical system	• products utilising the electrical systems	• improved lifecycle energy efficiency and reduction in e-waste and associated costs
• an education program to develop creativity and artistic expression	• the number of people or organisations undertaking the program	• innovation, human development and societal wellbeing, knowledge and cohesion

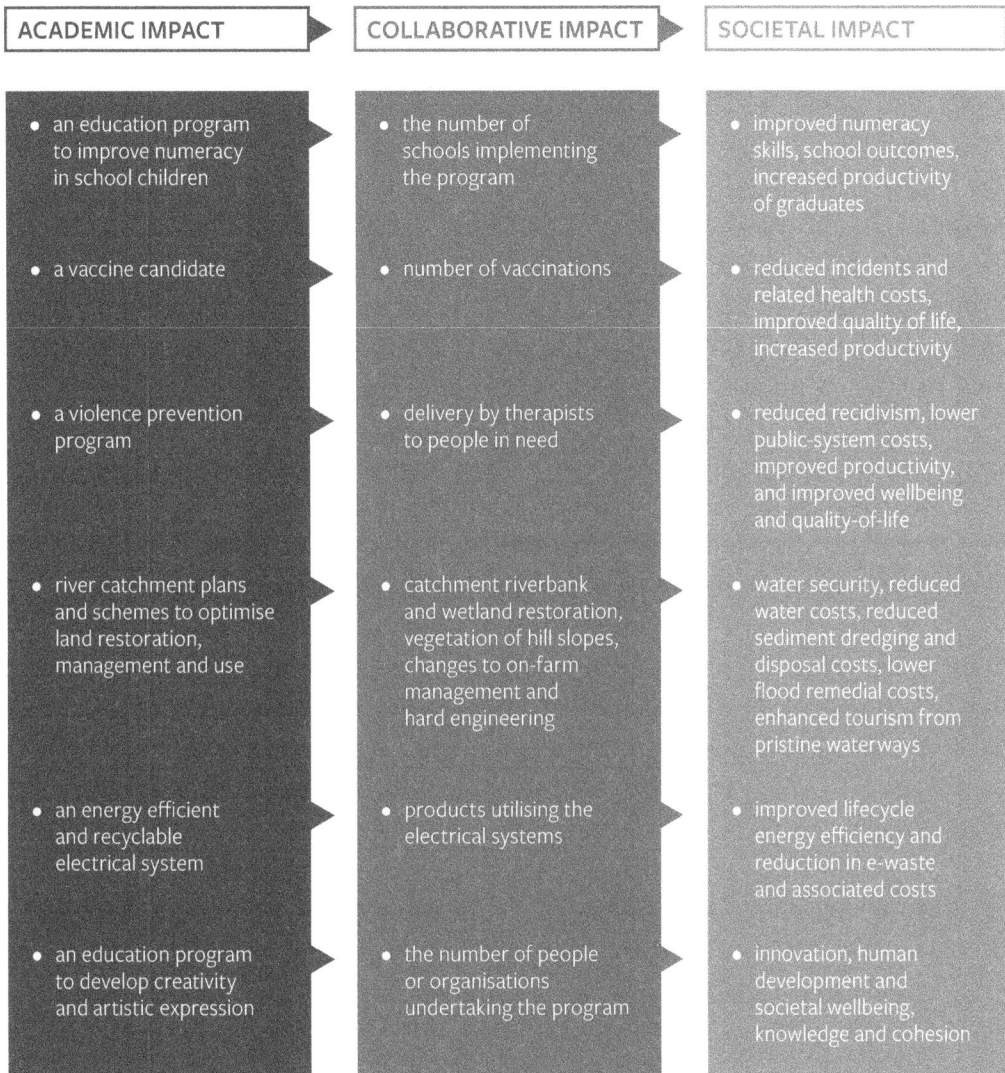

TABLE 1: EXAMPLES OF SPHERES OF IMPACT

Proposition 2

The second proposition states: If the potential for great societal impact is high, so too is the likelihood of collaborative impact from academic impact.

An example is again useful to explain this proposition, using the vaccine candidate shown in the table. Typically, a long-term, at-risk, multi-million-dollar investment is required to develop a safe and efficacious vaccine candidate and take it to market.

Vaccinations can cost a modest amount per person to deliver, but across a national or even larger population the cost of investment can climb into billions of dollars. In such a case, and here we pare back to the basics, we must ask what it is that supports such a long-term, at-risk investment and allocation of resources.

Treating the outcomes of a disease may incur costs of tens of thousands of dollars per person. The eradication of that disease, or a significant reduction of its effect through vaccination, can save healthcare systems a significant multiple of what it costs to develop and provide a vaccine overall, and enable a healthier and therefore more productive population to contribute so much more to society.

The overall societal benefits are profound. It is the potential of such immense societal impact that justifies the long-term at-risk investment in the development and provision of vaccines. One need look no further than the response to Covid-19 to observe how profound the socio-economic benefits can be from a successful vaccine.

Like the first proposition, the second proposition holds regardless of the diversity of underpinning disciplines. The greater the potential societal impact the greater the likelihood of collaborative impact from academic impact.

Proposition 3

The third proposition states: While the delivery of societal impact can be provided within the confines of universities, partnerships and collaborations with third parties (collaborative impact) are required to truly maximise societal impact.

In other words, a key component of maximising societal impact involves ensuring that the most people get the most benefit from utilising an education program, product or service. Partners and collaborators are integral to ensuring that this occurs.

Extending our vaccine example, without having suitable partners outside the university domain to expedite the effective rollout of vaccines around the world, the greatest societal impact could not materialise. Putting it another way, keeping a vaccine within the confines of a university to deliver (and I concede that this is unlikely) strictly rations the overall benefits that can otherwise be derived.

The third proposition, like the previous two, also holds true regardless of the diversity of underpinning disciplines.

APPROACH TO DERIVING IMPACT

If the three propositions are accepted, universities can most effectively galvanise action across disciplines by utilising the following three-pronged axiomatic approach to direct efforts toward deriving impact.

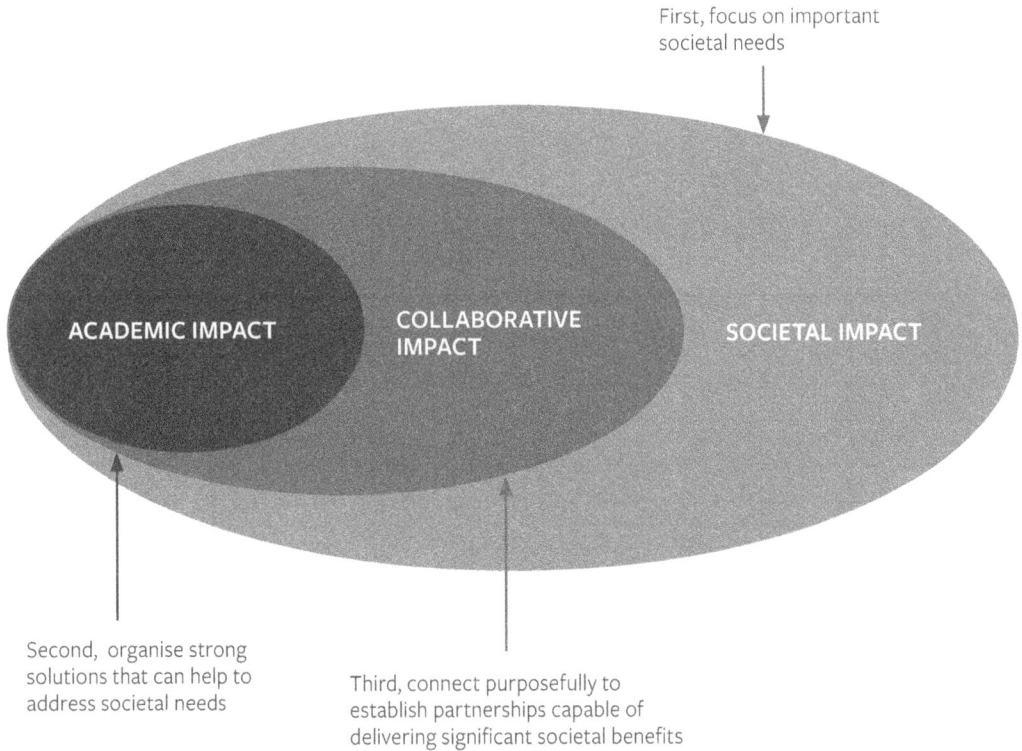

First, focus on important societal needs

SOCIETAL IMPACT

COLLABORATIVE IMPACT

ACADEMIC IMPACT

Second, organise strong solutions that can help to address societal needs

Third, connect purposefully to establish partnerships capable of delivering significant societal benefits

FIGURE 2: APPROACH TO DERIVING IMPACT

The first axiom dictates that universities must focus on the nature of significant societal needs. Only then, and this is the second axiom, can universities' resources be best directed toward developing solutions (e.g. tangible education programs and research outcomes) that address those societal needs. Using the third axiom, universities must include in their solutions to societal needs those partners and collaborators necessary so the most people in need obtain the benefits of the solutions.

Once the nature of societal needs, university offerings and collaborative partners are determined, universities must then join these dots and purposefully connect each component (or axiom) with another to establish the best arrangements that facilitate the delivery of the greatest societal impact possible.

Traditionally, most universities' efforts have focused predominantly on maximising academic impact. This focus is driven by the reality that the best-quality education programs and outstanding research outcomes attract quality students and build reputations attractive to leading educators and researchers. And, without question, this remains a critical component of the value of universities.

Another aspect of delivering impact can be located at some universities, where significant investment has been made into identifying the elements of academic impact that have commercial potential and then translating them through collaborative impact. This so-called 'technology transfer' or 'commercialisation' has yielded mixed results to date. The mixed results may be due to universities narrowly framing their approach around discovery and then looking for problems those discoveries can address, rather than tailoring solutions for identified and well-understood societal needs.

Therefore, the challenge for universities is to suitably position education programs and research activities as knowledge capital in a value chain, with the active intent of maximising the translation of outputs into impact. This requires a shift in perspective away from traditional approaches. The spheres-of-impact approach is key to this shift as it helps universities to investigate, understand and articulate the nature of societal issues; explore the unforeseen and unexpected possibilities alongside intended outcomes; and identify and understand end-users of education programs and research projects much earlier in the process of program and project planning.

ARTICULATING PURPOSE

Understanding the spheres-of-impact framework helps universities craft their purpose. With a strong sense of purpose, universities can galvanise shared action. By continually considering the following three questions, universities can work towards consistently articulating purpose:

> Question 1: What is the societal need?
> Question 2: How do we create solutions?
> Question 3: How do we liberate benefits?

The successful delivery of quality education programs generates high levels of expertise among graduates, or within organisations that can contribute to society. The development of impactful research outcomes provides solutions to needs and wants in society; however, only through the broadest utilisation of education programs and research outcomes by end-users in the community do the most benefits materialise. The value to society can be profound.

Delivering profound socio-economic benefits is *the* university value proposition. It is the reason for public funding and support for universities. To thrive, universities should therefore seek to continually maximise 'societal impact', from 'academic impact' through 'collaborative impact'. This is a common purpose for universities seeking to deliver socio-economic benefits for our world.

A well understood direction (framed around the north stars) coupled with purpose (framed around the spheres of impact) helps a university establish intent, an important aspect of setting organisational direction. The development of a framework to achieve intent now comes into play and is the focus of Chapter 3.

KNOWLEDGE-CAPITAL VALUE CHAIN

'The only real voyage of discovery consists not in seeking new landscapes but in having new eyes.'

—Marcel Proust

KEY THEMES

- Exploring suites of resources, addressable markets, and paths-to-markets

- Identifying market segments available to universities to be addressed, and delivery mechanisms to be utilised

- Understanding the knowledge-capital value chain and determining types of engagements

- Understanding the knowledge-capital value chain, the development of core strategies, and resource allocation decisions

It is intent that galvanises shared action across a university. This calls for a core strategy[1] that sets the framework for achieving intent. How universities make sense of ways to achieve this intent first requires an understanding of the knowledge-capital value chain and its three key constituent parts, namely (1) the nature of universities' underlying resources, (2) the market segments they address, and (3) the various delivery mechanisms that can be utilised. These constituent parts are not unfamiliar; indeed, they are common to all universities and acknowledged as staples of the domain of tertiary institutions. What makes them key in this context is the way they are perceived by universities in times of change and uncertainty.

To follow on from the consideration of a university's north stars and spheres of impact, an appreciation of the constituent parts of the knowledge-capital value chain and what these can offer when shaping a core strategy is an important next step towards the aim of deriving impact, starting with a closer look at the nature of resources.

NATURE OF RESOURCES

The underlying suite of resources available to universities sets them apart from many other organisations in today's business world. This suite can be condensed into three main categories, deployed by all universities to create solutions for society. Here we are talking about the potent mix of knowledge, research capabilities and innovations.

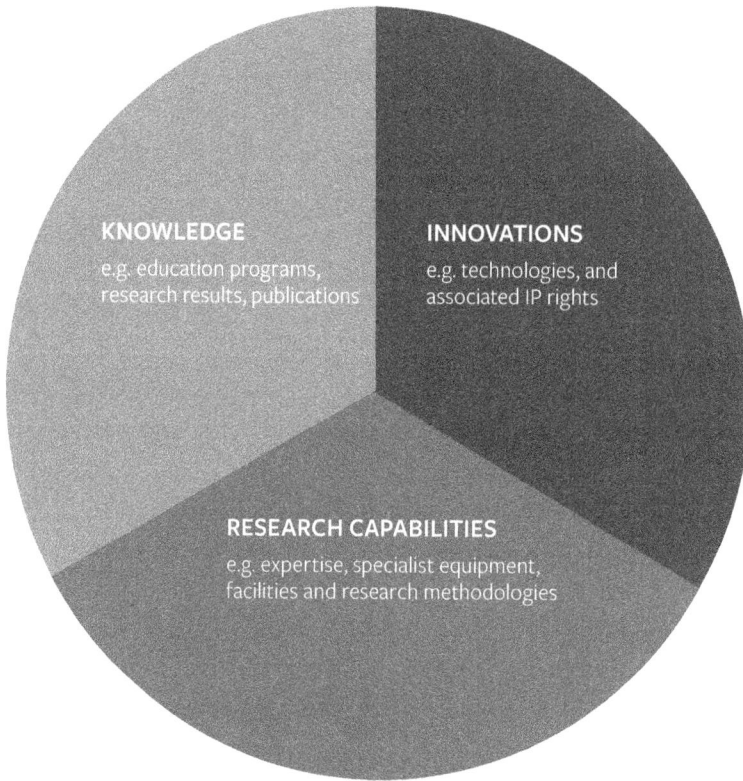

FIGURE 3: NATURE OF RESOURCES

Knowledge

For all universities, core business involves the delivery of education programs that are relevant to the needs of students and the wider community. Quality research informs and instructs, and is part of a knowledge base that underpins the provision of quality education programs. A university's ability to provide evidence-based, high-quality education programs and research outcomes[2] contributes to immense socio-economic benefits and a key competitive advantage.

Research capabilities

Research capabilities available to a university typically consist of expertise (e.g. residing with its academic staff), research facilities and equipment, and research methodologies (e.g. systems, processes, techniques, methods). The breadth of capabilities within a university that can be applied individually or collectively to solve complex problems also provides universities with considerable competitive advantage. The research capabilities of universities underpin both the creation of knowledge (above) and innovations (below).

Innovations

Universities undertake research that can result in innovations; typically, novel technologies, and new or unique products, services, processes or designs. For example, innovations may include a new vaccine or drug candidate, new electrical system, novel device, new material, and so on. Intellectual-property rights (e.g. patents, trademarks, and industrial designs) are often associated with novel innovations, shoring up competitive advantage.

MARKET SEGMENTS

Considered examination of the nature of resources helps to identify the addressable market segments available to a university. In the case of *knowledge*, education programs are delivered to large numbers of students and consumers, both domestic and international, and can also include school leavers; mature, full-time and part-time students; and people from within a broad range of disciplines and fields of endeavour (e.g. social sciences, physical sciences, life sciences, environmental sciences, the arts). There is also growing demand from organisations for specialist education programs to meet the needs of their workforces. This emergent market segment increasingly calls on universities to bring their expert knowledge to bear in the workplace, enabling employers and employees to up-skill, retrain and build professional capacity. An understanding of consumer and organisation segments and how to target them effectively is clearly critical.

Research capabilities often enable universities to work for or in partnership with organisations to supply solutions to problems, or advance their products and services to the wider community. Therefore, the addressable market segments for research capabilities typically involve organisations within industry, government and not-for-profit sectors. Here, too, universities require a clear understanding of organisation and consumer-market segments and how to target them.

Innovations from universities most commonly require further development to become, or be part of, viable products or services. Therefore, the 'markets' for innovations are often existing or new businesses that can further develop innovations for eventual delivery and sale to end-users. However, there can be circumstances where innovations are converted by universities into products and services that can be repeatedly sold to end-users or consumers (increasingly common with social enterprises). Here, again, a clear understanding is needed of organisation and consumer market segments and how to target them.

DELIVERY MECHANISMS

As the addressable market segments for knowledge, research capabilities and innovations differ, so too do the approaches to those market segments. This leads us to the third aspect of the knowledge-capital value chain that must be considered when shaping a core strategy, that of delivery mechanisms. This ultimately informs the likely pathways and approaches to those key market segments for a university.

Focusing first on *knowledge*, most education programs are delivered directly to students by universities using widely recognised systems and modes, incorporating online and face-to-face methods. In uncertain environments, however, it is also important for universities to be nimble and source programs from third parties, or engage third parties to deliver programs. Internal units (e.g. schools, faculties, groups) are often established to deliver education programs, and universities can also establish specialist units (let us call them 'enterprises') that are capable of repeatedly selling knowledge-based products or services to consumers. Importantly, as market segments include consumers and organisations, both business-to-consumer (B2C) and business-to-business (B2B) approaches are required.

While *research capabilities* can be accessed in many ways, they are typically acquired directly by third parties (e.g. industry, government and other organisations) in need of solutions to problems. This often involves the articulation of those problems and the ways to address them, meaning B2B approaches are again involved.

Innovations are typically advanced together with third parties (existing organisations or start-ups) through development into end products or services, followed by commercial sale. The associated activities around this delivery mechanism are often referred to as 'technology transfer' or 'commercialisation'. Collaborations are often involved, with revenue generated by commercial sales (or other forms of consideration) shared between the parties. The translation of innovations predominantly involves B2B approaches; however, in situations where products or services may be repeatedly sold to end-users, this may involve B2C approaches.

Therefore, for universities to thrive they must be proficient at both B2C and B2B approaches when delivering their offerings. They must understand that delivery mechanisms depend upon the nature of the underlying resources, the different market segments, and, crucially, the paths-to-markets and partners that can and must take very different directions. Once this understanding is established—with that goal of shaping a core strategy—fit-for-purpose engagements, through which impact can be derived, can be considered.

TYPES OF ENGAGEMENTS

Given the diversity of resources, market segments, paths-to-markets and partners, and delivery mechanisms, it is clear that universities also need to develop appropriate and flexible engagements if they are to maximise impact. These engagements can include translational research partnerships, consultancies, commercial research contracts, licences, new venture-establishment or social enterprises (as vehicles to deliver products or services), professional education and training agreements, joint ventures, corporate-wide partnerships, and so on.[3] The engagements often involve various combinations of resources and partners, and may involve combinations of delivery mechanisms.

The following diagram illustrates the numerous and diverse engagements that facilitate the pathways from academic impact to societal impact, covering virtually all elements and aspects of academic endeavour.

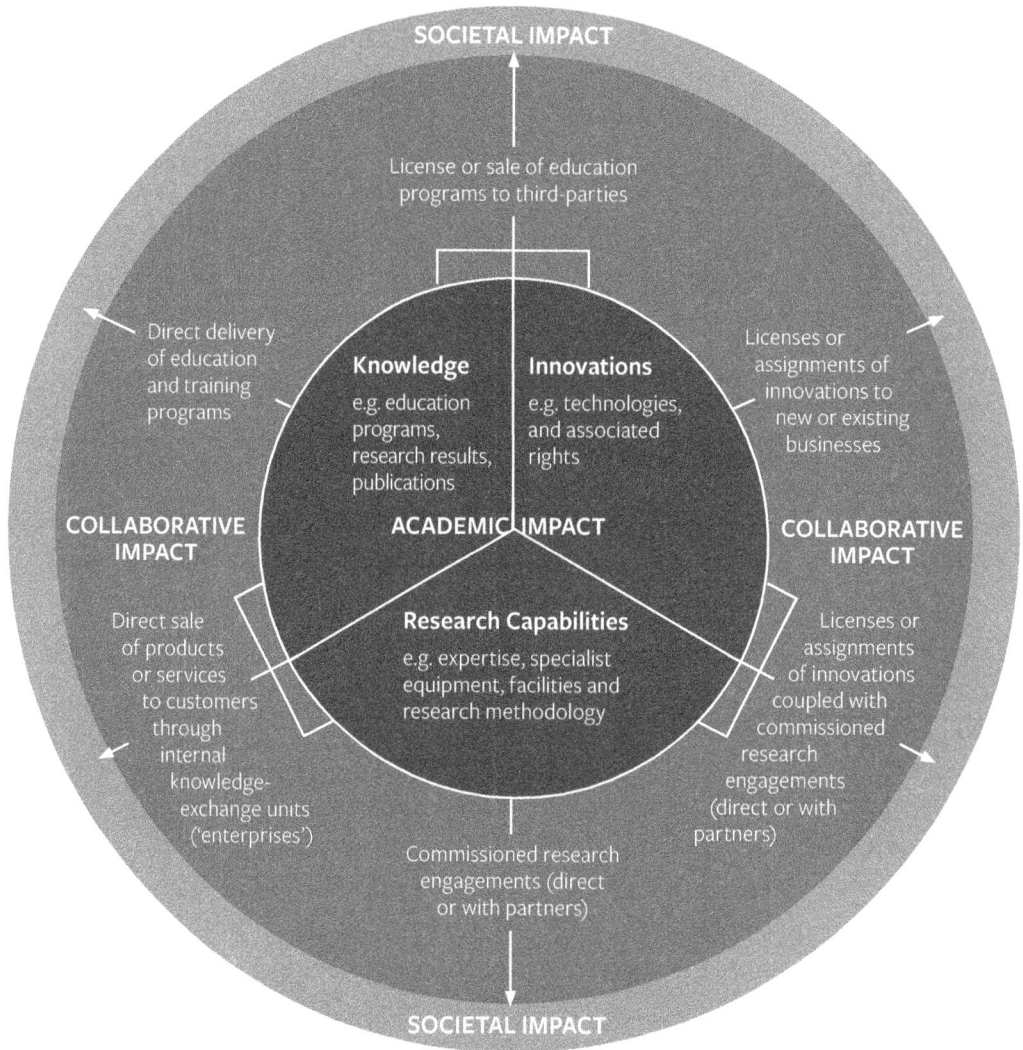

FIGURE 4: TYPES OF ENGAGEMENTS

FIRST THE VALUE CHAIN, THEN THE TYPE OF ENGAGEMENT

When shaping a core strategy that helps a university to derive impact, there can be a strong temptation to focus predominantly and prematurely on the types of engagement; however, this tendency must be resisted by universities truly seeking to derive impact. Universities must first understand the nature of the knowledge-capital value chain in shaping a core strategy and making associated strategic allocations of resources before determining the types of engagements to utilise. This sequence, and not the reverse, is a critical step toward ensuring impact from universities is maximised. This point cannot be overemphasised, as explained below.

Here the three-pronged approach that is central to understanding a university's spheres of impact is coupled with this understanding of the knowledge-capital value chain. This enables a university to proactively determine ways of utilising all of its assets, and consider how knowledge, research capabilities and innovations may converge in collaboration and partnership with external organisations in order to deliver the greatest impact possible.

Less nuanced approaches tend to focus on the types of engagement at the expense of the attention that must be given to the knowledge-capital value chain in the first place. If deriving impact is a key goal, it is paramount that strategies are in place to ensure that the most people in need are able to utilise the products or services a university and its partners offer. The strategies and resource allocation decisions that meet this overarching goal then determine the types of engagement.

A particular type of engagement (e.g. start-up, licence, joint venture, or some other form of deal structure) should not prescribe the best way to maximise societal impact. Doing this would be like choosing a vehicle before you know the terrain to be travelled. A university, with a multitude of options in a dynamic environment, must be guided in its business decisions by an understanding of the knowledge-capital value chain, and the associated strategies and strategic resource allocations.

FORWARD STEPS

In summary, universities can shape a core strategy through an understanding of the knowledge-capital value chain: the nature of underlying assets, differing markets and paths-to-markets, and delivery mechanisms. Continually considering the following questions additional to those posed earlier (Chapter 2, Spheres of Impact) can help universities shape core strategies to achieve intent:

> Question 1: What are our underlying assets?
> Question 2: What are our market segments and paths-to-markets?
> Question 3: What delivery mechanisms yield the greatest impact?

Through this process, it will be evident that universities can deliver an array of benefits to targeted consumers, such as students or organisations in the private and public sectors, either directly or in partnership. Given the diversity at play, and the rapidly changing environments in which they operate, universities must therefore develop effective ways to ascertain needs; build matching value propositions; and arrange flexible, fit-for-purpose approaches to maximise impact. And when setting organisational direction, universities must also discern which viable opportunities to pursue and which to pass up. Working within a confined resource envelope means it is not possible to address everything or be all things to all people. It is also necessary to consider an opportunity spectrum, which is the focus of Chapter 4.

Chapter 3 Endnotes

1. It is important here to differentiate between *shaping* a core strategy and the more complex task of *establishing* a core strategy, the latter endeavour beyond the remit of this book.
2. New knowledge generated through research can also manifest in peer-reviewed publications, available to all. There is ample evidence illustrating the tremendous benefits the dissemination of knowledge contributes to society.
3. There are more sophisticated variants than provided in this text, which will be covered in a subsequent publication.

OPPORTUNITY SPECTRUM

'Put first things first and we get second things thrown in; put second things first and we lose both first and second things.'

—C.S. Lewis

KEY THEMES

- Deciding which opportunities to pursue

- Determining how to position a university competitively to maximise impact

- Allocating resources strategically; deciding which opportunities to pursue and in what order

- Recognising different operational segments and where the opportunities lie

Universities must increasingly make judicious and far-reaching choices about the opportunities and possibilities that present. No longer can universities aspire to be everything to everyone; business decisions must address the question of which consumers and markets to chase, which programs or services to offer, and exactly which partnerships to pursue. These are hard decisions that require clarity of thought about how to use the wealth of resources available to the university. These are the moments when universities demonstrate that they are in tune with their public mandates, and they are best understood by exploring the nature of the decisions that universities—large, complex organisations—must make in relation to allocation of resources.

A RESOURCE-ALLOCATION CHALLENGE

Universities offer a diversity of programs, products and services to an array of consumers, such as students, and organisations like government and industry-based collaborators. And, like most other organisations, a relatively modest proportion of opportunities taken up by universities contribute the most significant social, cultural, economic or environmental benefits. To illustrate the complexity of this resource-allocation challenge, Figure 5 uses cumulative revenue[1] (vertical axis) obtained by a university from a suite of engagements ranked from the smallest (left-hand side) to largest (right-hand side).

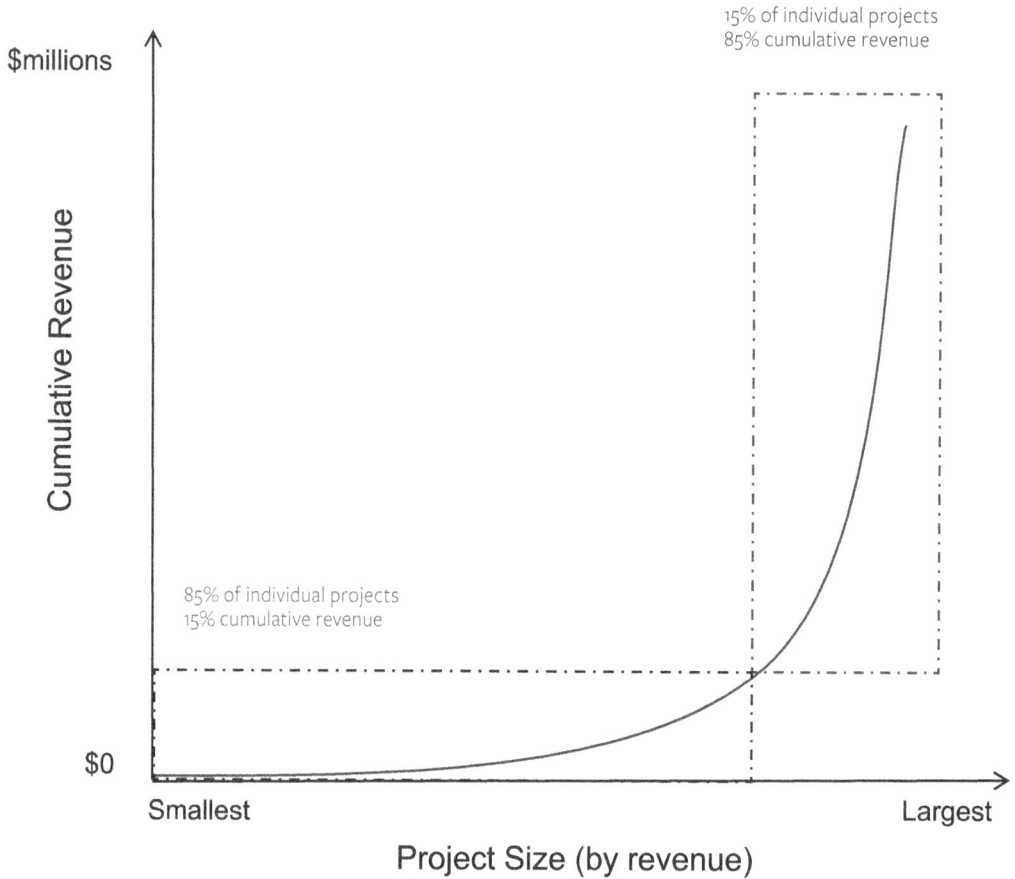

$millions

Cumulative Revenue

15% of individual projects
85% cumulative revenue

85% of individual projects
15% cumulative revenue

$0

Smallest

Largest

Project Size (by revenue)

FIGURE 5: A RESOURCE ALLOCATION CHALLENGE

This Pareto Principle-like issue is one not unfamiliar to most universities. In this case it shows that around fifteen percent of engagements are associated with around eighty-five percent of cumulative revenue. These proportions can of course vary depending on the nature of the activities (e.g. funding associated with various categories of student enrolments, versus funding associated with grant applications, versus funding associated with commercial partnerships). Despite these variations, the major challenge for universities is to focus on the opportunities likely to be most impactful when deciding on allocation of resources, those fifteen percent, say, of opportunities that deliver the greatest impact. In dynamic environments that are dealing with restricted resource envelopes, this is an imposing test for universities globally.

MEETING THE CHALLENGE

To maximise impact, universities must be proactive and ensure that resourcing is structured so they can capitalise on opportunities with the promise of significant impact. This approach helps universities to discern their opportunity spectrum, and in turn optimise resource allocation. Such attention to allocation of resources allows other interactions without this significance of impact to be managed in a facilitative and efficient way, and without unduly absorbing available resources. It requires being adept at making decisions about (1) positioning competitively, matching consumer needs to competitive strengths, (2) prioritising which opportunities to pursue, and in what order, and (3) allocating resources in a strategic manner to enhance likelihood of success.

Positioning

Understanding the nature of resources and how they can best be utilised to deliver impact helps to identify a spectrum of opportunities that may be pursued. Universities must therefore learn to be proficient at identifying and developing education programs, products and services ('offerings') that provide superior value propositions for stakeholders, and in ways that cannot be easily matched by competitors, or met by alternatives in a changing environment. If not, a university's overall efforts are diluted and its outcomes impaired.

It is important to consider the nature of a market—aggregate demand within it, various causal forces acting on it—as well as the strengths and weaknesses relative to the competition. In this regard, it is also important to note that a university comprises organisational factors, a set of levers potentially utilised to directly control or influence the market. Organisational factors include the underlying assets described earlier (Chapter 3, Knowledge-Capital Value Chain), as well as other factors like engagement model, operating model and implementation model (which will be covered in more depth in Part II of this book).

There are various situational factors to consider, which include market forces, industry structure and competitors. Situational factors tend to be outside a university's direct control.[2] It is the combined effects of organisational factors and the various situational factors that lead to consumer, customer or partner responses.[3]

Let's briefly discuss some of the parameters that may be considered in this context, using Figure 6. It is clear that attractive markets matched to competitive strengths offer opportunities that are more likely to succeed (as represented in the top right-hand quadrant of the diagram). Large numbers of consumers with compelling needs (e.g. students) or high-growth markets (e.g. healthcare) tend to represent such opportunities. Attractive customers often involve large organisations that can afford to have a major need addressed.

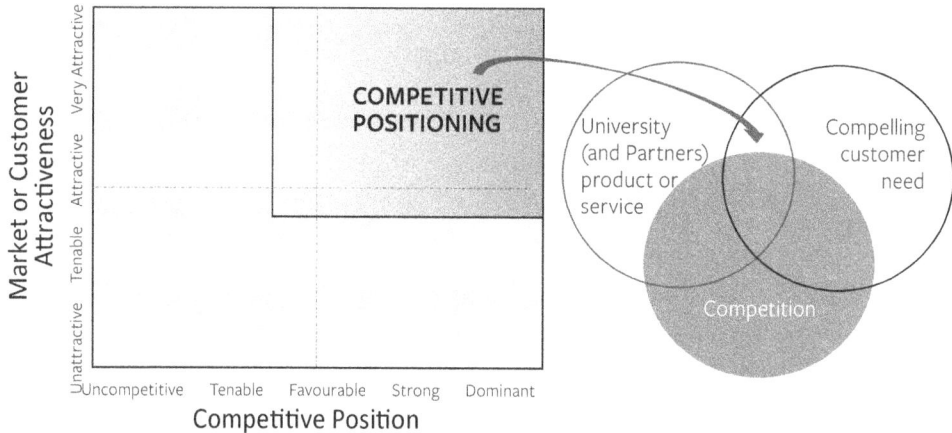

FIGURE 6: COMPETITIVE POSITIONING

It is important that universities persist in areas of considerable capability that can address such needs better than competitors and alternatives when required. Solutions to societal needs often involve multi-disciplinary and multi-party approaches. Multiple and interconnected causes can underpin major needs and therefore solutions rarely sit within the remit of a single organisation. Here a focus on the totality of resources (internal, and with partners) can be utilised to address an identified societal need. For example, evidence-based interventions can be coupled with trusted service providers to offer a better solution than those of the alternatives or competitors.

Clearly defined target groups with needs or problems that require solutions represent opportunities. Key targets can be societal issues that are a priority for the public sector (e.g. chaotic families, homelessness, recidivism, mental health, poor lifestyle choices, disability, out-of-home care). Evidence-based interventions coupled with trusted service providers that offer better solutions than the alternatives are keys to success. Considerable capability that is complementary to the capability of partners and collaborators is of major interest.

Prioritising

The decision-making process for universities must also determine which opportunities qualify for advancement. This process of prioritisation requires a university to make choices from the spectrum of opportunities available. The application of both outward-looking criteria (market based) and inward-looking criteria (organisation based) can help with making these decisions. Figure 7 (overleaf) illustrates a process, and key decision criteria.

```
          ┌─────────────────────────────────┐
          │   UNIVERSE OF OPPORTUNITIES     │
          └─────────────────────────────────┘
                          │
                          ▼
          ┌─────────────────────────────────┐
          │      MARKET QUALIFICATION       │
          └─────────────────────────────────┘
                          │
                        PASS
                          │
                          ▼
          ┌─────────────────────────────────┐
          │     OFFERING QUALIFICATION      │
          └─────────────────────────────────┘
                          │
                        PASS
                          │
                          ▼
          ┌─────────────────────────────────┐
          │     PRIORITY OPPORTUNITIES      │
          └─────────────────────────────────┘
```

FIGURE 7: PRIORITISING DECISION CRITERIA

Building on the spheres-of-impact framework and the knowledge-capital value chain detailed in previous chapters, universities must ensure that they understand the end-user needs; determine if the market sectors are strategically desirable; and identify realistic paths to market, including suitable partners and collaborators. If these factors are well understood, opportunities advance to the next stage. Those opportunities for which these factors are not well understood should not be prioritised.

Next, and in addition to market-based criteria, universities must also ensure that the requirements of their organisation as a whole are likely to be met. Invariably this also involves (1) determining whether or not a university's reputation is likely to be enhanced by the opportunities, (2) whether the university can offer a competitive-value proposition, and (3) whether or not the likely consideration (e.g. fees, funding, milestone payments, revenues) is sufficient to warrant the allocation of university resources. Those opportunities that are likely to meet all three requirements form priority opportunities.

Returning to the competitive positioning illustrated previously, the prioritisation of opportunities tends to fall into four major segments, as illustrated in Figure 8.

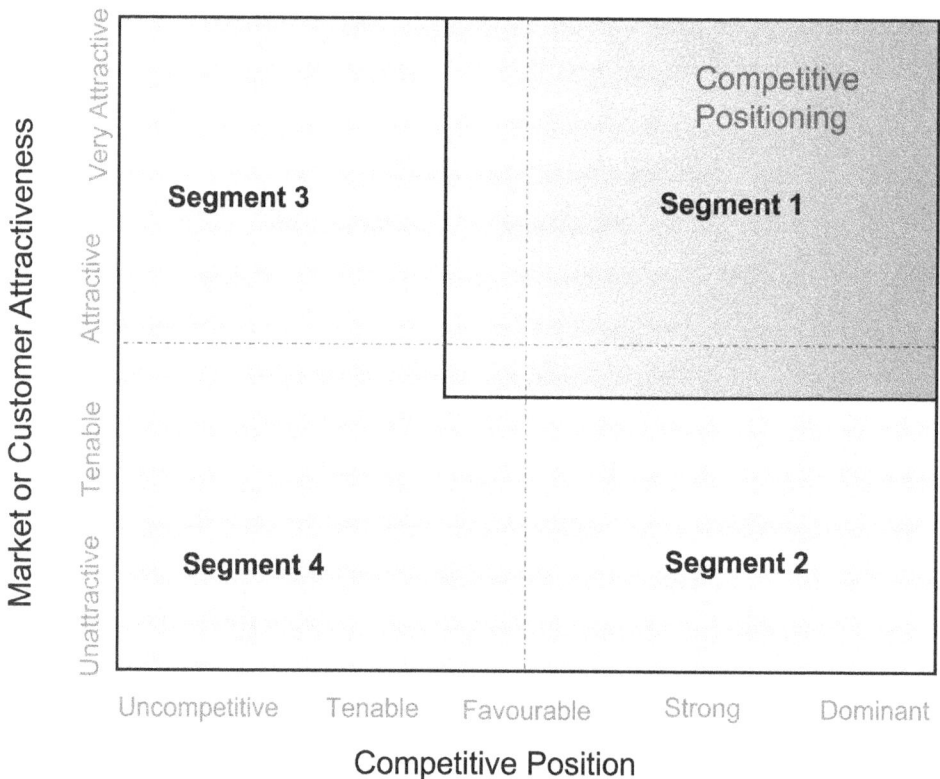

FIGURE 8: SEGMENTING FOR RESOURCE ALLOCATION

Attractive and very attractive markets or customers, coupled with strong or dominant competitive positions (segment one) should be prioritised.

Strong or dominant competitive positions tied with unattractive or tenable markets or customers (segment two) are unlikely to attract sufficient consideration to warrant prioritisation.

Targeting attractive and very attractive markets or customers with uncompetitive and tenable competitive positions (segment three) are unlikely to be successful; and typically results in unwarranted resource absorption, is unlikely to enhance university reputation and should not be prioritised.

Activity that targets unattractive markets with uncompetitive positions (segment four) clearly should be avoided.

Allocating resources

The process of positioning and prioritising opportunities helps universities hone organisational direction and make more informed investment or resource-allocation decisions. From a set of prioritised opportunities, those with the best chance of successfully delivering impact should have the most resources and investment allocated to them. Accordingly, universities need to build capabilities and competencies that enable them to make these informed investment and resource-allocation decisions. Five commonly utilised methods are described below.

Superior offerings: Uniqueness or superiority of offerings build capability and influence universities' differential advantages. They are typically the most positive factors contributing to success. Pricing of offerings is also important. A high price with no competitive advantages to a student or partner is obviously a significant barrier to success. Accordingly, for each priority opportunity, affirmatively answering the following questions gives confidence that resources should be allocated to advancing the opportunity:

- Uniqueness: Does the university offering differ substantially from competitors?
- Superiority: Is the university offering superior in terms of quality, performance, cost and efficiency?
- Newness: Is the university offering novel and hard to replicate?
- Importance: Is the university offering vital to a student's or partner's competitive advantage and not readily substituted?

Success factor analysis: Knowing the likelihood of success of a new product or service development enhances competency in decision-making around resource allocation. This can be achieved using assessment models that focus on (1) product or service-related factors (as described previously under the subheading *superior offerings*), (2) external environment (as described previously under the subheadings *positioning* and *prioritising*), and (3) internal environment (how matched the available resources are to delivering the offering to the external environment, and how easy it is to fill any capability gaps).

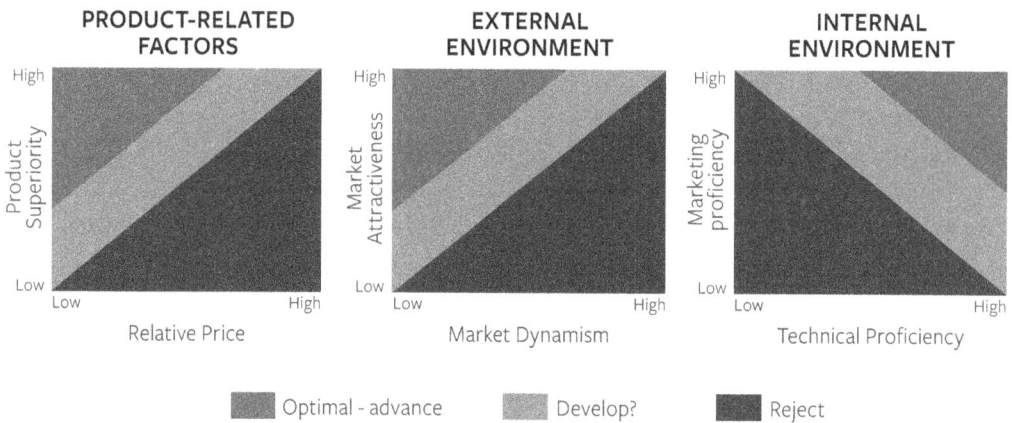

FIGURE 9: SUCCESS FACTOR ANALYSIS

The method illustrated in Figure 9 focuses on the factors that most affect product success and the issues that impinge on an organisation's ability to successfully implement an opportunity.[4] Most methods tend to involve a high degree of subjective judgement. Nevertheless, utilising the models across a portfolio of opportunities permits a comparative analysis and therefore helps to identify those more worthy of investment than others.

Activeness: An investigation and understanding of current and historical experiences can assist in resource allocation and related decision-making. Universities will have staff with varying degrees of collaborative activities and track records. Similarly, universities will have partners with whom significant business occurs, and target partners with whom they wish to do (more) business. Segmenting by staff and partner activeness can inform the level and nature of support that should be provided, as illustrated in Figure 10.

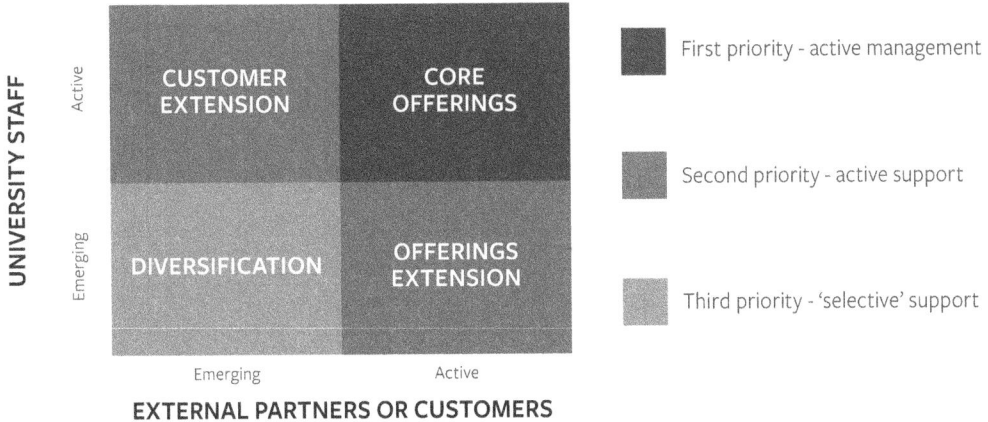

FIGURE 10: SEGMENTING BY ACTIVENESS

Active staff are those that are experienced at undertaking large-scale collaborative activity. They have strong track records and established networks that can be successfully leveraged. Emerging staff are those that have undertaken some, but not extensive, collaborative activity. They are at an earlier stage of building track records and establishing networks than active staff.

Active partners are those that undertake significant levels of business with a university (in terms of number, size, or range of engagements). They trust the university and are happy to work with the university. Emerging partners are those that have undertaken some initial business with the university. They are testing the university's ability to deliver offerings and are building working relationships with its staff.

Active management of core offerings (the combination of active staff and active partners, as depicted in Figure 10) commands, not surprisingly, the most resource allocation. However, the analysis can also help shape growth opportunities by focusing on ways to offer active staff to emerging partners (customer extension), or emerging staff to active partners (offerings extension), or by expanding reach through diversification, although this tends to be the most challenging path because both staff and partner development are required.

Technology diffusion: A university may have innovations or technologies that require further investment before they are of interest to partners. Assessing offerings based on size of investment, probability of success, and expected value can help judge likely viability and optimise resource allocation accordingly.

There are various useful models to assess probability of success and the expected value of early-stage technologies. A commonly utilised model is the technology-diffusion model. Technology diffusion relates to the rate at which new ideas and technologies are absorbed or diffused into the market or community. The technology-diffusion model attempts to make predictions about the likely uptake rate of new ideas by assessing various attributes of an offering (e.g. relative advantage, complexity, compatibility, perceived risk, trial-ability, and communicability) and applying some rough empirical rules to make estimations.

Most models tend to involve a high degree of subjective judgement, but utilising the model across a portfolio of opportunities permits a comparative analysis, and therefore helps to identify innovations that may be more worthy of investment than others.

Offering size: Given the breadth of resources available to a university, the nature of projects can be quite varied. Segmenting projects by size can also inform the allocation of resources to priority opportunities. There are two broad operational segments relevant here and these are indicated in Figure 11 comparing cumulative revenue with opportunities for impact, which is revisited here.

The first segment (indicated by the dark-grey-dashed box) comprises large collaborations, and invariably involves the provision of favourable or dominant competitive offerings to attractive markets. Universities need to determine ways to ensure that most available resources are allocated to support these partnerships and engagements.

The second segment (indicated by the light grey-dashed box) involves smaller engagements and, like the other, also results in impact. However, judicious allocation of resources toward supporting this segment is required since the impact is likely to sit at the lower end of the scale. It is noteworthy, however, that smaller engagements often blossom into larger ones, as relationships, track records and experience are built over time. Accordingly, this operational segment cannot be ignored, nor left unattended.

A third operational segment can exist and involves supporting uncompetitive offerings: those that are unlikely to be successful. Focusing on this segment results in the diversion of available resources away from supporting impactful opportunities. The process of positioning and prioritising opportunities can help mitigate this.

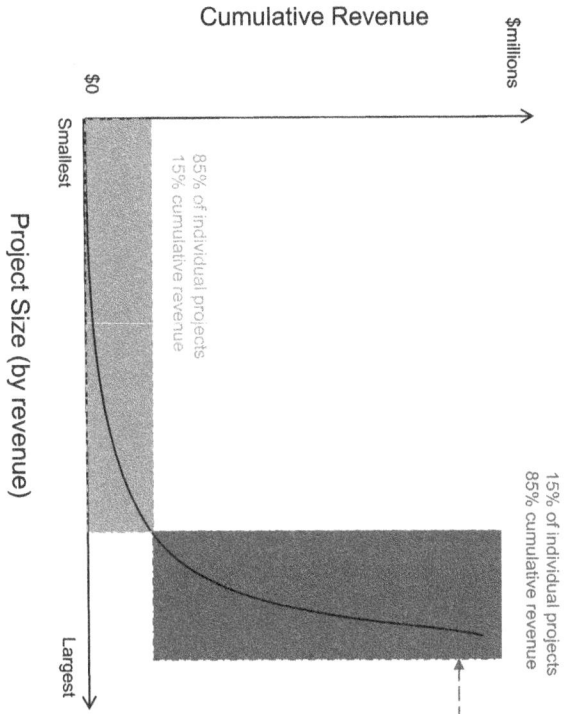

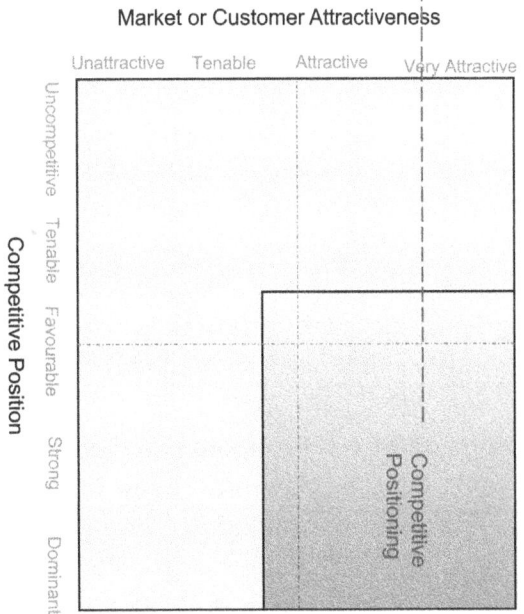

FIGURE 11: SEGMENTING BY OFFERING SIZE

Cumulative Revenue

$millions

$0

Smallest

85% of individual projects
15% cumulative revenue

15% of individual projects
85% cumulative revenue

Project Size (by revenue)

Largest

Market or Customer Attractiveness

Unattractive   Tenable   Attractive   Very Attractive

Uncompetitive

Tenable

Favourable

Strong

Dominant

Competitive
Positioning

Competitive Position

DISCERNING AN OPPORTUNITY SPECTRUM

Universities currently operate and will continue to operate in a world of flux. Opportunity spectrums, thus, can only be dynamic entities. Accordingly, decisions about competitive positioning and prioritisation must be made continually so the focus is consistently directed into attractive market segments and leveraging key areas of strength. The principles detailed in this chapter are therefore a process to be applied rather than a static plan.

Mapping opportunity spectrums is an everyday, ongoing process that informs strategy. As the opportunity spectrums change, so too do strategies evolve. By discerning opportunity spectrums, universities can pursue those opportunities that are consistent with their direction, purpose and core strategies, and are likely to derive the most impact from available resource envelopes. Continually considering the following questions can help universities in this regard:

> Question 1: Is the consumer or organisational need well understood?
> Question 2: Is the market segment strategically desirable for the university?
> Question 3: Is the university's offering superior to competitors or alternatives?
> Question 4: Will the university's reputation and finances be enhanced?

In summary, universities should focus resources on those segments in which they are currently active and successful. This allows them to leverage existing opportunities that are of strategic importance—where there are identifiable and realistic pathways in each segment—to partners or directly to consumers (e.g. students, partners or collaborators). Universities must have a clear understanding of the benefits they provide to their consumers and be proficient at offering valuable outcomes, and universities must also work with reputable partners in keeping with their overall mission to maximise societal impact. The process of positioning and prioritising enables universities to allocate appropriate resources to those opportunities that have the best chance of delivering impact.

In Part I of this book we pieced together a conceptual framework for organisational direction. The main goal has been to connect a university's *intent*, established through a combination of direction and purpose, with its *focus* through an understanding of the knowledge-capital value chain and a prioritised spectrum of opportunities in environments of flux.

Also key to deriving impact is building an organisational character capable of anticipating opportunities, and creating and providing solutions that address associated needs. Full and considered attention is given to this in Part II.

Chapter 4 Endnotes

1. It is acknowledged that cumulative revenue (e.g. fees, royalties, funding) is not a particularly good proxy for funding associated with student enrolments, nor is it a good measure of overall impact. However, it can be used to illustrate the key resource-allocation challenge that universities face.

2. Please note that aggregate demand within an addressable market is typically an uncontrollable situational factor, as is competition. Consumer demand is based on customer need, and hence to dramatically change demand a university must be capable of dramatically affecting needs. This tends to limit a university's impact on the basic market. However, a university can affect the brand, or the solution, or the program, product or service customers adopt, and therefore the rate of adoption and market share.

3. Common mistakes are (1) to focus on organisational factors as if they are the sole cause acting on the market (i.e. ignoring market forces, industry structure and competitors), and (2) to focus only on organisational factors and competitors as if they are the sole causes (i.e. ignoring market forces and industry structure).

4. An investment-success-factor analysis was developed from work undertaken by Dr Robert Cooper in the 1990s at McMaster University in Canada.

PART II

ORGANISATIONAL CHARACTER

'The old river in its broad reach rested unruffled at the decline of day, after ages of good service done to the race that peopled its banks, spread out in the tranquil dignity of a waterway leading to the uttermost ends of the earth.'

—Joseph Conrad, 'Heart of Darkness'

CHAPTER 5

CRITICAL PROFICIENCIES

'Order and simplification are the first steps towards mastery of a subject.'

—Thomas Mann

KEY THEMES

- Identifying the factors to be mastered to achieve organisational direction - the 'critical proficiencies'

- Understanding the pivotal role of critical proficiencies in designing organisational character capable of implementing organisational direction

- How to 'curate' offerings and 'shape' mutually beneficial and enduring engagements that 'deliver' great societal outcomes

Quite unlike any other social institution, universities are charged with ensuring that the most people possible gain the greatest benefits from their expert knowledge, research capabilities and innovations. It is not a burden to be underestimated or sidestepped in any way; it remains a seminal part of any university's DNA. The opening four chapters laid out the multidimensional approach required to achieve this goal and derive impact from universities. In Chapter 5, we consider the specific university activities that must be carried out in-house to reach these lofty and worthy goals, activities underwritten by an unequivocal expertise, without which universities cannot effectively manage the exchanges that ultimately lead to societal benefits. Now comes the point in the process where a well-intentioned university asks: How do we get this done?

IDENTIFYING CRITICAL PROFICIENCIES

Along with *setting* organisational direction, careful consideration must also be given to the *implementation* of organisational direction, and *aligning* various organisational activities so that great outcomes are achieved. Organisational character is required to support the achievement of organisational direction. How universities get a sense of what is required at this stage starts with identifying those key factors that universities must master to achieve their organisational directions. These can be called 'critical proficiencies'.

To understand a university's critical proficiencies and why and how they are relevant, it is helpful here to recall the spheres-of-impact framework explored in Chapter 2. There, it is proposed that to derive impact from universities, an outward focus on major societal needs is required, along with an ability to shape education programs and research outcomes to address those needs. To truly ensure that our communities derive the greatest socio-economic benefits from each opportunity, it was proposed that collaborations with many other organisations are required. Through the prism of the spheres-of-impact framework, it becomes clear that universities deliver great societal impact from their academic impact through collaborative impact.

Building on the spheres of impact, it can be asserted that universities must become proficient at curating opportunities, shaping successful partnerships, and working together with other organisations to deliver benefits. This important operational link between the spheres-of-impact framework and the critical proficiencies is shown in Figure 12 below, following which each individual proficiency is outlined in more depth.

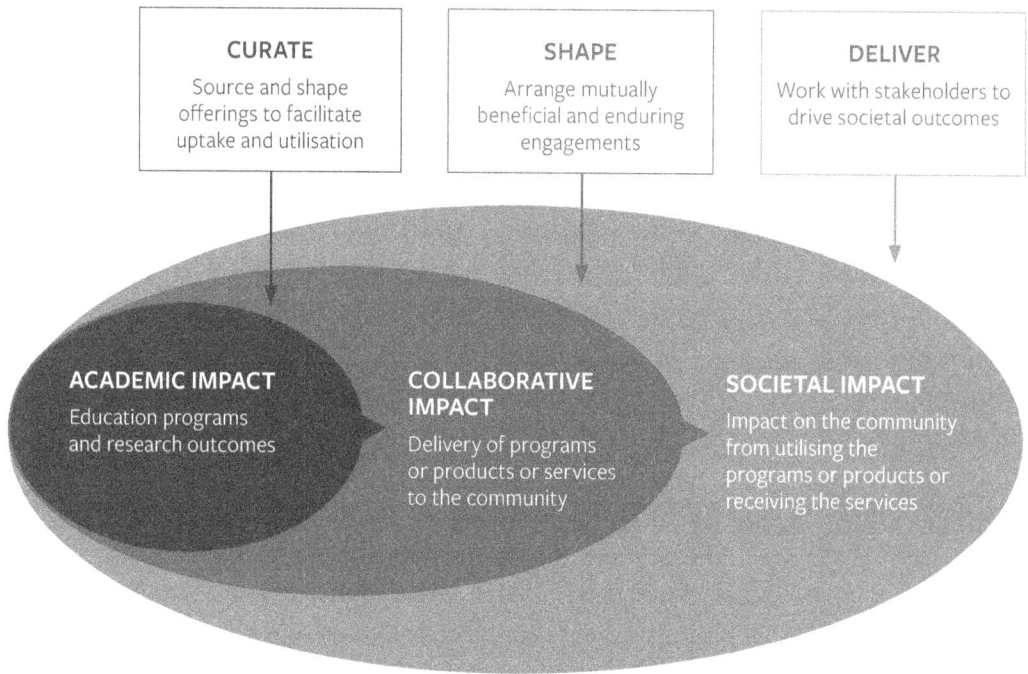

FIGURE 12: CRITICAL PROFICIENCIES

PROFICIENCY 1: CURATE

Organisational direction sets the context within which the curation of opportunities occurs. For each north star, a university must derive a spectrum of opportunities it can pursue and to which resources can be strategically directed. All universities must therefore become specialists in sourcing, selecting and organising institutional offerings that are likely to facilitate uptake and utilisation by others.

The challenge here is to identify potential or intended outcomes, and end-users of scholarship and research, early in the process of program and project planning, and then design approaches that maximise the likelihood of translatable outcomes. The key is to target and go after attractive opportunities with competitive offerings through the suitable alignment of associated activities and resources. The outcome of this alignment is the conversion of knowledge into products and services that, through innovation, make tangible and measurable contributions to social and economic wellbeing.

In short, by being proficient at curating opportunities, universities can start to successfully derive impact. Three key requirements that a university must master to curate opportunities are:

1. Imparting a common understanding of organisational direction and engendering a sense of shared purpose (north stars, spheres of impact, knowledge-capital value chain, and opportunity spectrum)
2. Orienting, activating and motivating key academic staff to develop opportunities and advance external partnerships
3. Judiciously deploying resources to advance programs, products and service offerings to a stage where uptake is probable.

To position offerings competitively, universities must become adept at examining internal environments (e.g. organisational resources such as knowledge, innovations, and research capability) and external environments (e.g. markets served, paths-to-markets, and competitive landscapes). This examination, which requires purposeful engagement with internal and external stakeholders, is especially pertinent when curating opportunities. Purposeful engagement is the fulcrum for mobilising resources to deliver profound societal impact (and is a crucial standalone topic that is discussed in the next chapter).

Similarly, all offerings involve key academic staff, along with partners, as the providers of solutions to societal issues. Universities must therefore become adept at establishing an operating model that empowers, assists and supports academic staff to curate opportunities. Further, the curation of opportunities involves a wide range of activities involving people, and universities must develop ways to bring its people and partners together collectively to derive socio-economic benefits. An implementation model is clearly a critical component of success.

PROFICIENCY 2: SHAPE

For successful partnerships to occur, universities must be able to initially source potential or likely partners, and then establish value propositions for those partners and for themselves. There are three main aspects to this.

Partner-value proposition

First, as universities operate in competitive environments, the value propositions offered to partners must be differentiated, or be more valuable than alternatives in the marketplace. Such a value proposition exists when the benefits derived by a partner (which, conversely, are the benefits to be provided by a university) exceed what that partner is required to pay for those benefits (which, conversely, are the funds or consideration to be received by a university for providing the benefits). Typically, there are many external organisations (including other universities) offering bundles of benefits and price points to potential partners. Therefore, the ability to position offerings competitively, often through differentiation, is required on the part of universities.

Partnership-value proposition

Second, universities must also benefit from the partnerships, and must be able to do so in the context of competitive environments. The benefits received by a university from a partner (e.g. funds or other forms of consideration) must exceed the cost of providing the benefits (e.g. in the form of products or services) to that partner. If not, a partnership will not be enduring and therefore cannot sustainably deliver societal benefits. Operating in circumstances where universities cannot cover costs, or where provision of products or services is too risky, means that the likelihood of sustainable social dividend is low. In a competitive environment, an ability to shape partnerships that are on an economically sound footing is required on the part of universities.

University-value proposition

Third, entering engagements with third parties involves risks to a university. There are risks associated with an engagement itself (e.g. risk of financial loss), but also beyond an engagement and more broadly (e.g. risk of impaired reputation, impacting other university operations; or opportunity costs or forgone future revenue streams associated with, for example, impaired intellectual property rights). Risks may be mitigated, however, through judicious selection of partners, and the professional management of associated partnership terms and conditions. Universities must not only become skilled at positioning competitively and economically, but must also be adept at partner selection, articulating the scope of the partnership (i.e. what is to be provided) and negotiating and documenting the associated terms (i.e. the basis upon which provision occurs).

Accordingly, all universities must become proficient at shaping mutually beneficial and enduring engagements for socio-economic benefits to materialise sustainably. An exercise in moulding and forging an engagement with a partner—the capacity to shape—is another critical proficiency required by the university if impact is to be derived. Key requirements and activities that a university must master to shape enduring engagements include:

- Establishment of value propositions for the university and its partners
- Identification, assessment and attraction of key partners capable of supporting broad delivery and utilisation of products and services
- Flexible, fit-for-purpose and mutually beneficial deal structures.

With their stock rising in this context, the need for purposeful engagement, supporting operating model and implementation model, is again highlighted here.

PROFICIENCY 3: DELIVER

Only through the successful delivery of products or services to the community (and their utilisation by the community) can socio-economic benefits materialise. Deciding which opportunities to pursue, finding the best partners, and then structuring mutually beneficial engagements is achieved by the curation of opportunities and the shaping of engagements. But these are only two steps along the road to final delivery. Once an engagement is established and agreed upon, universities must also be adept at implementation, especially in the context of the aforementioned changing environments.

Internal and external environments change over time, introducing challenges and risks, and actual outcomes inevitably vary from expected outcomes. Moreover, because of the nature of exchange between universities and partners, the interests of both parties can diverge. Typically, there are shared returns (or benefits) and risks, and these need to be balanced between counterparties. Accordingly, universities must have expertise in critical elements of delivery, including risk-mitigation processes, contingency planning and project management. Unless universities deliver on the promise, their reputation and finances can be diminished, and ultimately the delivery of social dividends can be impaired.

Next, if universities are to truly drive socio-economic benefits along with their partners, they need to establish partnerships that are enduring. This requires universities to think of partnerships beyond the remit of one particular engagement. Enduring partnerships may involve the continual delivery of outcomes. They may involve scaled delivery models (over time) so that products and services can reach the broadest number of end-users in need. They may also involve a broad number of interactions across the full gamut of offerings (e.g. sponsored research, research collaboration, staff exchange, shared infrastructure, scholarships, student placements). Accordingly, to deliver greater benefits universities must have expertise in building sustainable and scalable partnerships, and partnership-management capabilities.

Finally, enduring partnerships also inevitably involve significant stakeholder management due to the multitude of parties that are involved when dealing with societal challenges. Stakeholders invariably involve those within universities and partners, but also those in the broader community. Universities must be adept at winning votes and working in harmony with many stakeholders to deliver long-term socio-economic benefits. Accordingly, universities must have expertise in key stakeholder relationship management to deliver greater benefits.

Key requirements and activities that a university must master to deliver impact include:

- Implementing the scope of the partnership and delivering agreed outcomes
- Building sustainable and scalable partnerships to expand the delivery of outcomes
- Managing and supporting partners and stakeholder relationships for long-term benefits.

Here, too, is evidence of the need for purposeful engagement, a supporting operating model, and an implementation model to deliver the products and services that drive long-term positive societal outcomes.

INTERCONNECTEDNESS OF PROFICIENCIES

Because the critical proficiencies are linked to the way socio-economic benefits are derived from universities, they are interdependent in their connection to one another; all three are required to maximise socio-economic benefits. This link is obvious if we consider what happens in the absence of any critical proficiency.

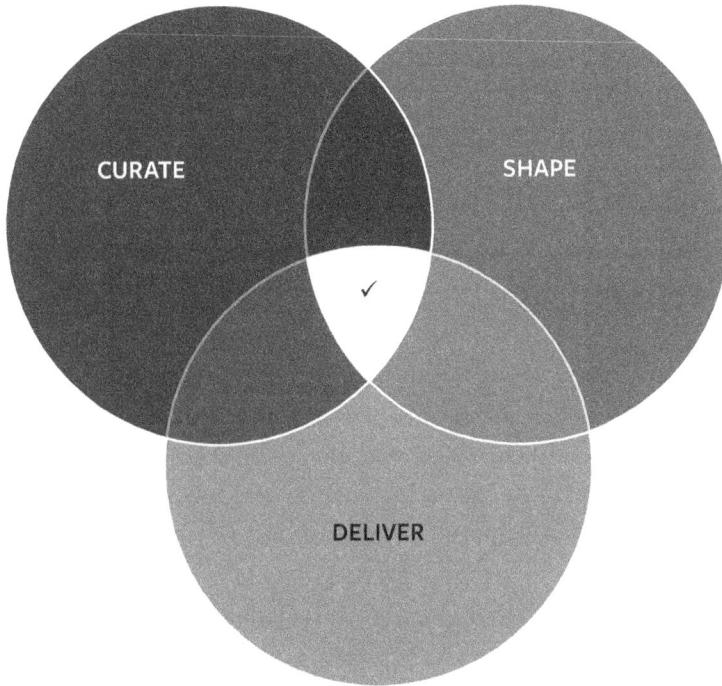

FIGURE 13: INTERCONNECTEDNESS OF PROFICIENCIES

For example, the curation of an offering and the delivery of the associated solution in the absence of mutually beneficial partnerships are unlikely to maximise socio-economic benefits. The offering's reach and supporting funding are likely to be rationed. Partnerships that are not mutually beneficial are unlikely to be sustainable and therefore unlikely to deliver major benefits.

Similarly, the curation of an offering, and the entering into of mutually beneficial partnerships but not delivering as expected, will not maximise socio-economic benefits. In this instance poor performance or unforeseen adverse events are present. This arrangement is also unlikely to be sustainable or deliver significant benefits.

Finally, delivering on mutually beneficial partnerships which are not aligned with organisational direction, future resourcing or overall best interests of a university, fall outside the province of maximising societal benefits from that university. In this instance, non-core business has been curated, and is unlikely to be supported in the long term.

DESIGNING ORGANISATIONAL CHARACTER

With an in-depth understanding of the three critical proficiencies, it is possible to design the organisational character (the engagement model, operating model, and implementation model) required to support the setting of organisational direction.

The critical proficiencies are the key factors that bind together organisational direction (what we will do) and organisational character (how we will do it) as illustrated in Figure 14 overleaf and explained below.

Through intent and focus, universities can articulate who they serve, why they are important, how they deliver socio-economic benefits, and what they offer and to whom. This helps determine what universities will do. Determining the activities that universities need to master to achieve their organisational directions helps to formulate the organisational character required for implementation.

Importantly (and not surprisingly), a change in organisational direction can precipitate a change in organisational character. Similarly, a change in organisational character can heavily influence the setting of organisational direction. Organisational direction and organisational character are inextricably linked. However, regardless of this interrelatedness and the constant changes to organisational direction or organisational character due to shifting internal and external environments, all universities that deliver impact consistently attain the three critical proficiencies, the glue that binds character with direction.

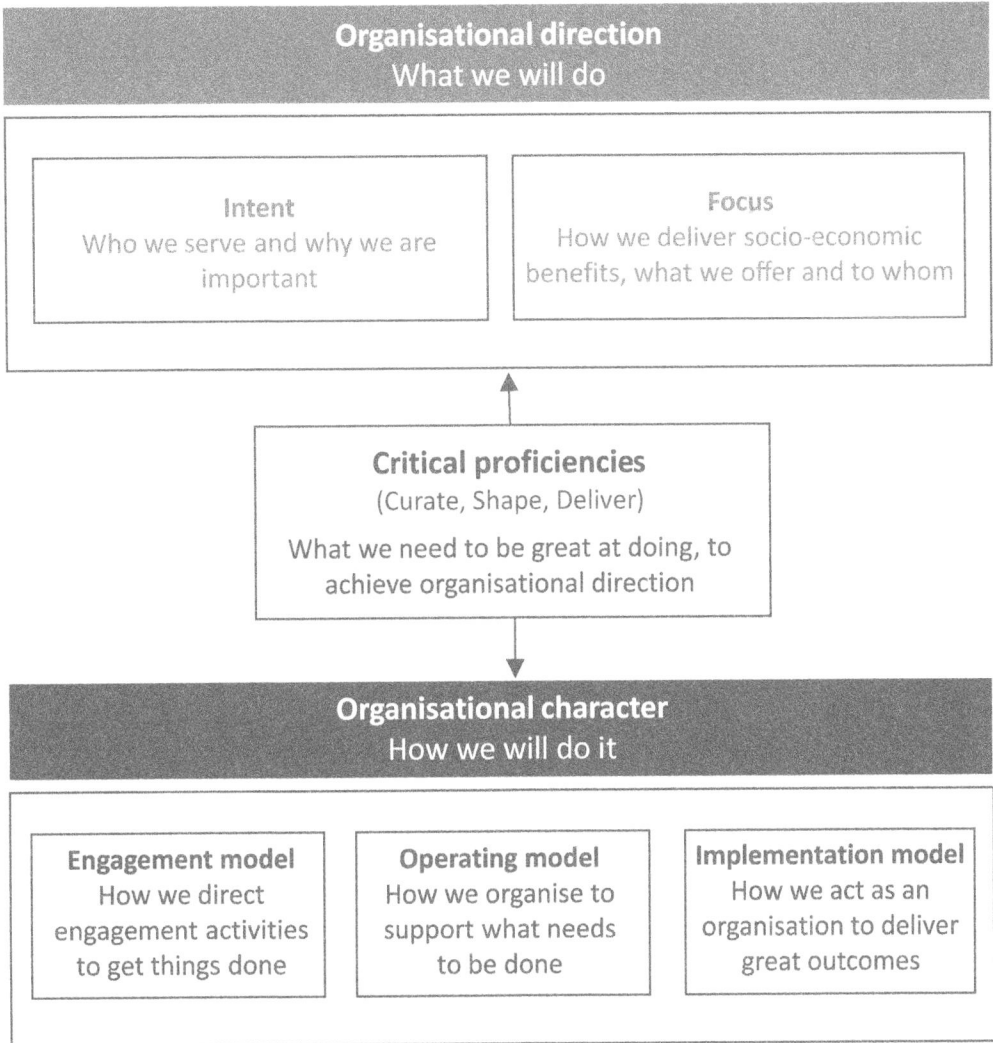

```
┌─────────────────────────────────────────────────────────────┐
│                  Organisational direction                     │
│                     What we will do                           │
└─────────────────────────────────────────────────────────────┘
┌─────────────────────────────────────────────────────────────┐
│  ┌──────────────────────────┐  ┌──────────────────────────┐  │
│  │          Intent          │  │          Focus           │  │
│  │  Who we serve and why we │  │  How we deliver socio-   │  │
│  │      are important       │  │  economic benefits, what │  │
│  │                          │  │  we offer and to whom    │  │
│  └──────────────────────────┘  └──────────────────────────┘  │
└─────────────────────────────────────────────────────────────┘

                    ┌───────────────────────────┐
                    │   Critical proficiencies  │
                    │   (Curate, Shape, Deliver)│
                    │  What we need to be great │
                    │  at doing, to achieve     │
                    │  organisational direction │
                    └───────────────────────────┘

┌─────────────────────────────────────────────────────────────┐
│                  Organisational character                     │
│                     How we will do it                         │
└─────────────────────────────────────────────────────────────┘
┌─────────────────────────────────────────────────────────────┐
│ ┌─────────────┐  ┌─────────────┐  ┌─────────────────────┐    │
│ │ Engagement  │  │  Operating  │  │  Implementation     │    │
│ │   model     │  │    model    │  │      model          │    │
│ │ How we      │  │ How we      │  │ How we act as an    │    │
│ │ direct      │  │ organise to │  │ organisation to     │    │
│ │ engagement  │  │ support     │  │ deliver great       │    │
│ │ activities  │  │ what needs  │  │ outcomes            │    │
│ │ to get      │  │ to be done  │  │                     │    │
│ │ things done │  │             │  │                     │    │
│ └─────────────┘  └─────────────┘  └─────────────────────┘    │
└─────────────────────────────────────────────────────────────┘
```

FIGURE 14: DESIGNING ORGANISATIONAL CHARACTER

Accordingly, the three critical proficiencies must become bellwethers for universities seeking to deliver socio-economic benefits for our world.

DEVELOPING CRITICAL PROFICIENCIES

Universities that thrive always create highly effective partnerships that are mutually beneficial. Together with partners, they develop effective solutions to meaningful problems and in turn deliver the socio-economic benefits our world needs. To thrive, therefore, universities must attend to the key proficiencies required to derive impact. Continually considering three questions can help with this goal:

> Question 1: How do we source offerings to facilitate uptake (curate)?
> Question 2: How do we arrange mutually beneficial engagements (shape)?
> Question 3: How do we work best with our partners and stakeholders (deliver)?

The answers to the above questions must be known across the breadth and depth of a university's organisational structure if it is to thrive, and a key activity here involves internal and external engagement, which must be carried out in a manner that is consistent with organisational direction. We move next to the first critical aspect of the required organisational character to derive impact: the engagement model.

ENGAGEMENT MODEL

'Knowledge is of two kinds. We know a subject ourselves, or we know where we can find information on it.'

—Samuel Johnson

KEY THEMES

- Engaging purposefully to gain the information required to make key decisions

- Garnering intelligence used for decision-making from both internal and external environments

- Understanding the key objectives of purposeful engagement

- Using channels of engagement that support the flow of valuable information and expert knowledge

Determining the best ways to maximise societal impact is challenging for universities that are operating with constrained resources in increasingly dynamic internal and external environments. It calls for strong decisions based on reliable information that has been garnered astutely and efficiently. Enhanced knowledge of the environment outside the university domain must be accumulated when deciding on the best partners with whom to shape enduring and productive partnerships to drive societal benefit. None of this can be achieved to the requisite level without engagement: the generative activities through which universities ensure that the correct information is at hand at crunch moments, so the right opportunity is embraced at the right time.

WHY PURPOSEFUL ENGAGEMENT IS IMPORTANT

Universities seeking to maximise societal impact invariably have an outward focus on major societal needs, and they shape education programs and research outcomes to address those needs. They also have the ability to work directly or in partnership with external organisations and key stakeholders to ensure that socio-economic benefits materialise from those programs and outcomes.

As a result, universities are presented with many different underlying reasons to not just engage but engage with purpose. These include garnering market intelligence and insights, building relationships and networks, creating buy-in through shared vision, fostering active support from key stakeholders, structuring flexible and sustainable partnerships, and working with partners to ensure that the most people in need have access to programs, products and services.

This diversity of reasons, coupled with the breadth of activities across a university, can make the nature and scope of engagements seem astonishingly complex, and can lead to disparate activities that are often ineffectual and can dilute overall effort. It is important, therefore, to appreciate the overarching objective of engagement from the outset. For example, is the major objective to (1) set organisational direction, (2) curate opportunities, (3) shape enduring partnerships, or (4) work with partners to deliver outcomes?

When the objective is clear, the purpose can be determined, and the purpose of engaging frames the questions to be answered, and sharpens the focus of the engagement activities required to answer them. This is an important step in progressing from reactionary to purposeful. By bonding the purpose of engaging with the foci of engagement activities, increasingly effective decisions and actions may then be taken, converting otherwise disparate engagement activities into purposeful engagement (or discarding them).

FIGURE 15: APPROACHING ENGAGEMENT PURPOSEFULLY

NATURE OF PURPOSEFUL ENGAGEMENT

In Chapters 1 to 4, we explored the ways universities can set organisational direction to maximise societal benefits, and in Chapter 5 we outlined the reasons why universities need to be critically proficient at curating opportunities, shaping partnerships, and delivering outcomes to achieve organisational direction. These four key objectives will now be utilised to unpack the nature of purposeful engagement.

Objective: Set organisational direction

If setting organisational direction is the objective, the key purpose of engagement is to *inform* decisions on direction using relevant and accurate information about both internal and external environments. Internal engagement helps to *examine* a university's resource profile (e.g. strengths, weaknesses, resource gaps), while external engagement is used to *seek* major trends, attractive markets, paths-to-markets, and competitive positions. To inform decisions effectively, a university must first examine internally and seek externally.

Internal- and external-engagement activities must also operate in tandem around a given purpose. If the purpose of engaging is to establish a university's north stars, there are various underlying questions that can only be answered through both internal- and external-engagement activities. Similarly, if the purpose of engaging is to discover a university's opportunity spectrum, a set of different questions needs to be addressed by engagement activities, both internal and external (along with the utilisation of various engagement channels to be canvassed subsequently).

This framing of the required engagement activities around a purpose (as illustrated in Figure 16) converts otherwise disparate activities into purposeful engagement. This theme remains a constant throughout the following figures (17 to 20) and aspects of engagement.

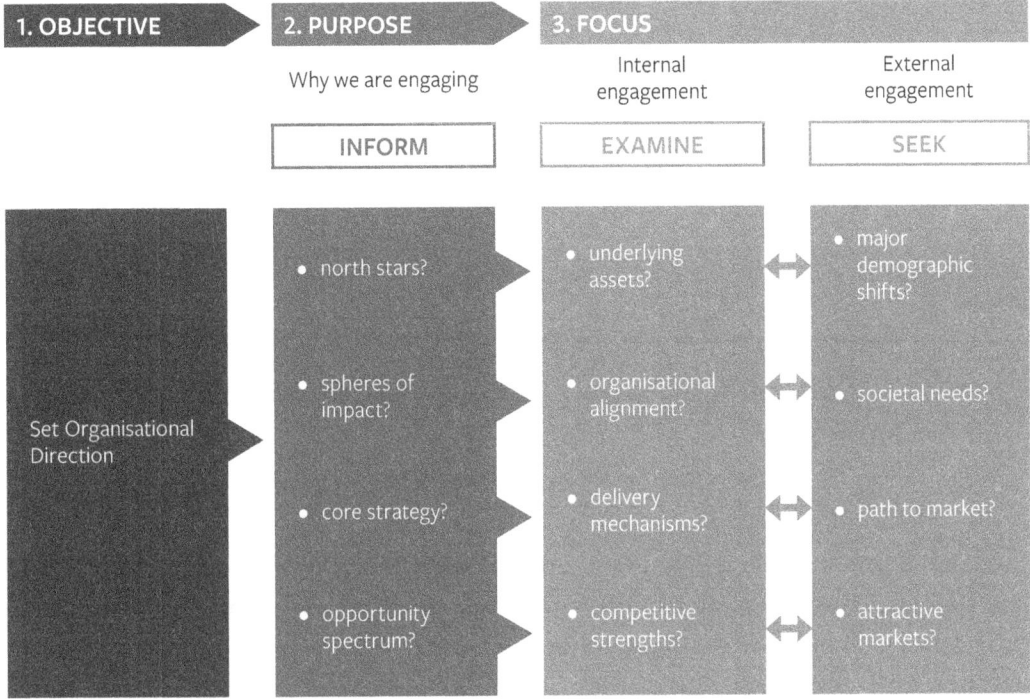

1. OBJECTIVE	2. PURPOSE	3. FOCUS	
	Why we are engaging	Internal engagement	External engagement
	INFORM	EXAMINE	SEEK
Set Organisational Direction	• north stars?	• underlying assets?	• major demographic shifts?
	• spheres of impact?	• organisational alignment?	• societal needs?
	• core strategy?	• delivery mechanisms?	• path to market?
	• opportunity spectrum?	• competitive strengths?	• attractive markets?

FIGURE 16: PURPOSEFUL ENGAGEMENT FOR ORGANISATIONAL DIRECTION

Objective: Curate opportunities

For universities to successfully derive impact, they must become proficient at curating opportunities. Here, the purpose of engagement shifts from *inform* to *enlist*, viz, the sourcing and design of offerings to facilitate uptake and utilisation. In essence, the engagement activities associated with curating opportunities are a starting point for the implementation of a university's organisational direction as it supports the development of a portfolio of tangible education programs and research outcomes that can address major societal needs.

The focus of external engagement is to *understand* the problems to be solved, while the focus of internal engagement is to *activate* the orientation and deployment of resources toward providing solutions to those problems.

Figure 17 illustrates purposeful engagement in the context of curating opportunities.

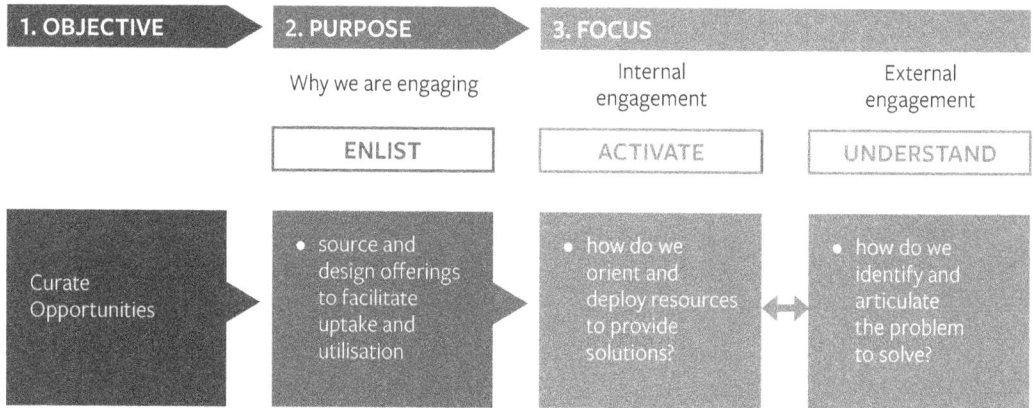

1. OBJECTIVE	2. PURPOSE	3. FOCUS	
	Why we are engaging	Internal engagement	External engagement
	ENLIST	ACTIVATE	UNDERSTAND
Curate Opportunities	• source and design offerings to facilitate uptake and utilisation	• how do we orient and deploy resources to provide solutions?	• how do we identify and articulate the problem to solve?

FIGURE 17: PURPOSEFUL ENGAGEMENT TO CURATE OPPORTUNITIES

Internal- and external-engagement activities are inextricably linked. Undertaking external engagement where a university has capability (and competitive position) increases the likelihood of impactful opportunities. Similarly, undertaking internal engagement with knowledge of the external environment (including competitive position) can lead to more effective resource allocation and be more likely to curate opportunities.

Objective: Shape partnerships

To ensure that the most people get the most benefit from education programs and research outcomes, universities must be proficient at shaping enduring partnerships. Here, the purpose of engagement shifts from *enlist* to *structure*, viz, shaping mutually beneficial and sustainable partnerships.

Internal-engagement activities are required to *craft* tangible offerings, which involves determining university approaches to solving problems, identifying the best combination of resources required to solve problems, assembling offerings, and determining the appropriate partnership terms.

External-engagement activities are required to *attract* the best partners. This involves exploring ways to work together, and using the process of due diligence to identify and select the best partners. Also relevant in this context is the shaping and justifying of offerings, and negotiating, documenting, and entering partnerships.[1]

Again, internal- and external-engagement activities are galvanised around purpose (here described as structure) and are fundamental to successfully shaping the partnerships required to derive societal benefits.

Figure 18 illustrates purposeful engagement in the context of shaping partnerships.

In this case, engagement activities support the business-development initiatives required to ensure that tangible education programs and research outcomes are capable of delivery to students and organisations. The engagement activities support the entering into of the portfolio of partnerships required for delivery.

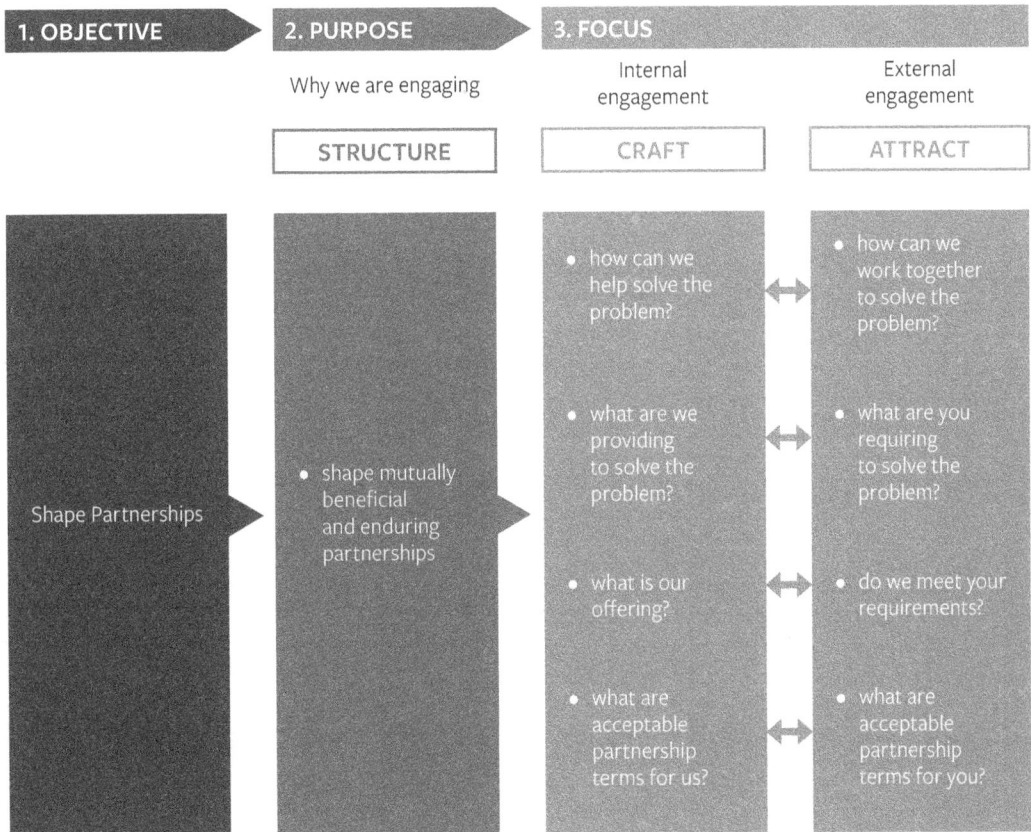

FIGURE 18: PURPOSEFUL ENGAGEMENT TO SHAPE PARTNERSHIPS

Objective: Deliver outcomes

Universities, along with their partners, must be proficient at delivering solutions to problems, whether that is through tangible education programs, research outcomes or innovations. This is how societal outcomes materialise. Here, the purpose of engagement shifts from *structure* to *perform*, ensuring that those most in need benefit from the provision of the solution.

Internal engagement is focused on *managing* to facilitate the successful delivery of the solution. External engagement is required to *leverage* outcomes, which not only ensures delivery but also often assists the partnership to scale so that more people in need of the solution are reached.

Again, the matching of internal and external engagement to the purpose (i.e. perform) is fundamental to successfully deriving societal benefits from universities.

Figure 19 (overleaf) illustrates purposeful engagement in the context of delivering outcomes.

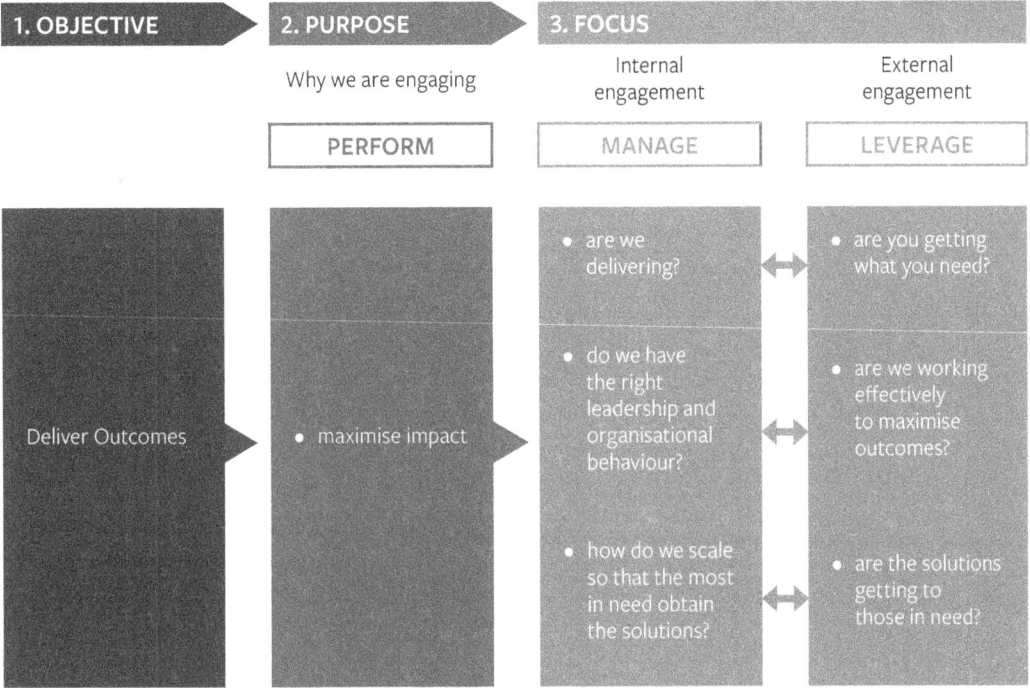

1. OBJECTIVE	2. PURPOSE	3. FOCUS	
	Why we are engaging	Internal engagement	External engagement
	PERFORM	MANAGE	LEVERAGE
Deliver Outcomes	• maximise impact	• are we delivering?	• are you getting what you need?
		• do we have the right leadership and organisational behaviour?	• are we working effectively to maximise outcomes?
		• how do we scale so that the most in need obtain the solutions?	• are the solutions getting to those in need?

FIGURE 19: PURPOSEFUL ENGAGEMENT TO DELIVER OUTCOMES

ORIENTATION OF ENGAGEMENT

It will be evident that some aspects of purposeful engagement have a strategic orientation and others a more operational orientation. Engagement activities with a strategic orientation, such as determining organisational direction and curating opportunities, help direct engagement efforts that have an operational orientation. Engagement activities with an operational orientation, such as shaping enduring partnerships and delivering benefits, help inform organisational direction and future engagement efforts.

This continual directing and informing, illustrated in Figure 20 (next page), demonstrates the inherently iterative nature of this process and the ever-evolving links between the various activities.

Strategic Orientation

Objective	Purpose of Engagement	Focus of Internal Engagement	Focus of External Engagement
Set Organisational Direction	'Inform'	'Examine'	'Seek'
Curate Opportunities	'Enlist'	'Activate'	'Understand'

Operational Orientation

Objective	Purpose of Engagement	Focus of Internal Engagement	Focus of External Engagement
Shape Partnerships	'Structure'	'Craft'	'Attract'
Deliver Outcomes	'Perform'	'Manage'	'Leverage'

Directs Engagement Effort

Informs Engagement Effort

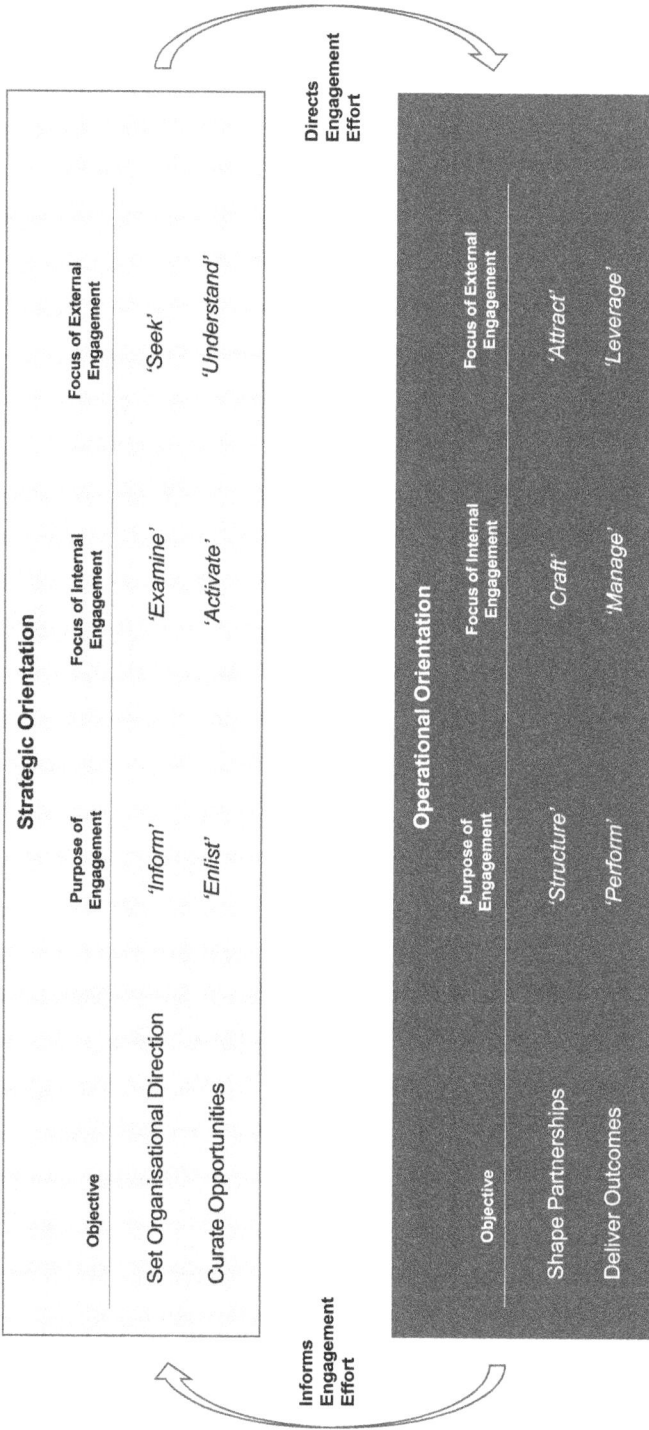

FIGURE 20: ORIENTATION OF ENGAGEMENT

While the outcomes from purposeful engagement differ, however, the approach to purposeful engagement remains the same, guided by an objective that is constant. This is all galvanised by a university's ability to direct and inform engagement activity in a coordinated manner, facilitated by the selection and use of appropriate channels of engagement.

CHANNELS OF ENGAGEMENT

A university can be described as a complex of diverse programs, products and services that are offered to an array of partners and consumers. In such a business context, engagement activities are, without question, a fulcrum for deriving great societal impact from universities. This is especially the case for organisations with defined resource envelopes that face unprecedented challenges of rapid and repeated disruption.

Moving on from purposeful engagement, we now give important thought to the support mechanisms for the engagement activities that can only be brought about through suitable avenues. These are the lines of connection, always live, always open, within the university complex; the myriad tributaries that support the flow of valuable information and expert knowledge as they reach past university perimeters to catchments beyond.

In effect, these are the channels of engagement utilised by universities to enable the internal and external engagement. In most cases, these channels will be recognisable and familiar, but considered thought is warranted when it comes to how they function in the university setting and how they serve university objectives. We start with an examination of internal-engagement channels.

Internal-engagement channels

The channels for internal engagement can be extensive, and can include face-to-face meetings, group workshops and peer-exchange programs (collectively utilised to build relationships); events, seminars and digital/online platforms (often used to increase awareness); strategic-planning sessions and concept-development workshops (applied to explore opportunities); and more formal internal meetings (to project manage and ensure outcomes consistent with agreed partnership arrangements).

In nearly all instances, face-to-face meetings involving academic staff are key to success. Academic staff possess high-quality knowledge of their fields of endeavour. They form a cornerstone of the offering process, and competitive offerings often involve teams of academic staff drawn from broad fields of endeavour. As educators, research experts or creators of intellectual property, university staff provide the solutions sought by partners and collaborators. They are integral to delivering solutions and, together with partners, socio-economic benefits.

This means that building internal relationships with and between key academic staff is clearly fundamental to success. Therefore, it is incumbent on universities to ensure that various channels are in place to maintain and increase awareness of organisational direction across the entire university, and to explore potential solutions to societal or organisational challenges. Those channels that inform academic staff of the various support services and programs available to them are also critical to the curation of opportunities, and the shaping of enduring partnerships.

Individual meetings may not always be practical to gain the necessary internal reach. In such circumstances, events, seminars, and digital/online platforms to present these opportunities are often utilised. On a more structured level, strategic-planning sessions and internal-concept workshops can be used to explore opportunities to articulate the nature of problems, shape associated solutions, and mobilise key stakeholders. Strategic-planning sessions can also be a useful platform when considering how best to leverage existing partnerships and relationships.

TABLE 2: INTERNAL ENGAGEMENT CHANNELS

OBJECTIVE	PURPOSE	FOCUS	INTERNAL ENGAGEMENT CHANNELS (examples)
To set Organisational Direction	Inform	Examine	• Face-to-face meetings • Group workshops • Strategic planning sessions
To curate opportunities	Enlist	Activate	• Face-to-face meetings • Internal events • Digital/online support • Seminars • Concept development workshops
To shape partnerships	Structure	Craft	• Face-to-face meetings • Internal workshops
To deliver outcomes	Perform	Manage	• Face-to-face meetings • Peer exchange programs • Project meetings and reporting

Drawing on the purposeful-engagement framework presented earlier, depicted in Table 2 are important channels of internal engagement matched to the objectives and purposes of engaging.

External-engagement channels

The channels for external engagement can be extensive, but may be broadly grouped into five main categories, namely (1) leveraging internal networks, (2) leveraging third-party networks, (3) digital networks, (4) expanding networks (by going out), and (5) expanding networks (by bringing in).

Experienced academic staff are always a good starting point for external engagement. Many staff are active within industry and government networks, with connections forged through the delivery of programs, products and services that create value. These are internal networks that can be leveraged by a university for external engagement.

In the same vein, external networks can also be leveraged by partnering with large national or international organisations that regularly win projects, by participating in peer-exchange programs (e.g. secondments of staff for periods of time to share knowledge and experiences), or by utilising specialist business brokers (particularly useful when engaging in international markets).

Digital networks—both internal and third-party platforms—offer an efficient way to showcase university resources, with targeted social media campaigns that drive traffic often key to success. There are many websites dedicated to brokering partnerships between universities, public-research institutes and industry. Some of these sites are supported by industry, government or philanthropic organisations and have varied business models (e.g. subscription based, or success-fee based).

OBJECTIVE	PURPOSE	FOCUS	EXTERNAL ENGAGEMENT CHANNELS (examples)
To set Organisational Direction	Inform	Seek	• Academic staff networks • University business networks • Internal websites • External websites • Tradeshows and conferences • Trade commissions and organisations • Business development roadshows
To curate opportunities	Enlist	Understand	• Academic staff networks • University business networks • External websites • Tradeshows and conferences • Business development roadshows • Commercial partners attraction programs • Strategic partnerships • Peer exchange programs • Third-party brokers • Piggy-backing (joint bids)
To shape partnerships	Structure	Attract	• Academic staff networks • University business networks • External websites • Tradeshows and conferences • Trade commissions and organisations • Business development roadshows • Commercial partners attraction programs • Strategic partnerships • Peer exchange programs • Third-party broker • Piggy-backing (joint bids)
To deliver outcomes	Perform	Leverage	• Commercial partners attraction programs • Strategic partnerships • Peer exchange programs • Third-party broker • Piggy-backing (joint bids)

There are also many government-based websites that showcase capabilities to international markets as part of economic-development agendas. Typically, these are associated with foreign investment, and trade organisations or departments overseeing industry-development and innovation initiatives. A simple internet search will reveal many.

On the ground, rather than online, networks can also be expanded by going out (e.g. business-development road shows, tradeshows, trade commissions) and by bringing in (e.g. hosting key industry partners on campus, or establishing industry advisory boards). The channels of engagement, therefore, must be varied in their formation and function.

Drawing again on the purposeful-engagement framework presented earlier, Table 3 depicts important channels of external engagement matched to key university objectives, associated purposes of engagement, and the focus of engagement activities.

PRIORITISING ENGAGEMENT

Both internal- and external-engagement activities are fundamental to deriving impact from universities. Equally clear is that universities cannot be everything to everyone. Accordingly, the discussion moves forward to the process of informing, positioning and prioritising opportunities. This involves combining clarity of purpose for engagement activities with, first, the nature of opportunity and, second, the operational segments.

In the case of the nature of opportunity, we revisit Chapter 4, where we explored how a university can discern its opportunity spectrum, which is essentially the process of matching university strengths to opportunities. Informed by its opportunity spectrum, a university gains an understanding of the nature of opportunity, allowing proactive engagement activities that can then be directed toward those opportunities and partnerships that are likely to yield the most socio-economic impact.

In the case of the operational segments, also discussed in Chapter 4, we retrace how the diversity of activities at any university necessitates different approaches and resourcing.

There are two major operational segments. The first is made up of the relatively small number of engagements associated with most of the cumulative revenue. This operational segment involves a proactive approach, significant internal- and external-engagement activities, and longer-term resourcing and investment to position opportunities for expansion and success. For this operational segment, the full gamut of internal- and external-engagement channels is utilised, with significant resource allocation warranted.

Long-standing relationships with third parties are a hallmark of this segment, along with multiple touch-points across organisations and the provision of multiple offerings, and it therefore requires customer-relationship-management approaches.

The second operational segment involves most engagements associated with a relatively small proportion of cumulative revenue. The diversity of engagements in this operational segment necessitates different approaches to, and resourcing of, associated activities. Relationships typically exist between individual university staff and third parties, involving the provision of a single line of service or product.

This segment requires efficient and effective support, and streamlined processes, and it should absorb much less resourcing and investment. With suitable channels in place, albeit with lower resource allocations warranted, within this segment a university can be well positioned to efficiently manage the business offering.

A third operational segment can exist; viz., supporting uncompetitive offerings that are clearly unlikely to be successful. This operational segment warrants little resource allocation toward supporting engagement and associated channels.

ESTABLISHING ENGAGEMENT

Through purposeful engagement, universities can best set organisational direction and be proficient at curating opportunities, shaping enduring partnerships, and delivering great socio-economic impact. Therefore, continually considering the following questions can help universities engage purposefully:

Question 1: What is the objective of engagement?
Question 2: What is the purpose of our engagement activities?
Question 3: What is the focus of our internal and external engagement?

In answering these questions, a university must also ask if it has the support structures in place for engagement activities to happen with the required purpose.

Through channels of engagement, universities strive to ensure that important information about the expertise and resources within the university is live and consistent, while also enhancing knowledge of external environments and associated opportunities. These channels, when set in place strategically, support and enable purposeful engagement.

Continually considering these additional three questions can help universities stay relevant and maintain supportive channels:

> Question 4: Are our engagement activities aligned with the opportunities that derive impact?
> Question 5: What channels best serve our purposeful internal engagement activities?
> Question 6: What channels best serve our purposeful external engagement activities?

Armed with a framework that enhances purposeful engagement and the utilisation of the appropriate channels for engagement, we move next to designing an operating model that can support the achievement of universities' organisational directions.

Chapter 6 Endnotes

1.   The nature of the exchanges between universities and partners, and the interconnected value propositions that must be established, are integral to establishing enduring partnerships (and will be the subject of another publication).

OPERATING MODEL

'The main thing is to keep the main thing the main thing.'

– Stephen Covey, American educator, author, businessman, and keynote speaker

KEY THEMES

- Establishing operating models consistent with overall organisational directions

- Aligning the central, core processes with critical proficiencies

- Understanding the role of enabling systems and how they support core processes

Delivering value is a complex endeavour for any university, and for larger institutions with a broad or diverse range of elements and disciplines the complexity can be multiplied significantly. The nature or effect of the endeavour is most efficiently understood with an operating model. With our singular focus on the university sector, the following definition of the operating model has been carefully selected and will be utilised here: a description of the processes, systems and functions required to deliver value to stakeholders.

For universities to derive impact successfully, the operating model must be consistent with overall organisational direction (Chapters 1 to 4) and must support critical proficiencies (Chapter 5). Its vital place in our framework for deriving impact is presented piece by piece in this chapter, starting with its components.

COMPONENTS OF AN OPERATING MODEL

The three key components of an operating model that derive impact from universities are (1) core processes, (2) enabling systems, and (3) organisational functions.

Core processes are the key actions required to deliver great societal impact. They must be aligned with the critical proficiencies, and they represent the linked actions required to derive societal impact. Enabling systems are the activities, programs and methods (resources) that enable the core processes to deliver value. Organisational functions are those areas within a university that provide the necessary professional services to support enabling systems and operations.

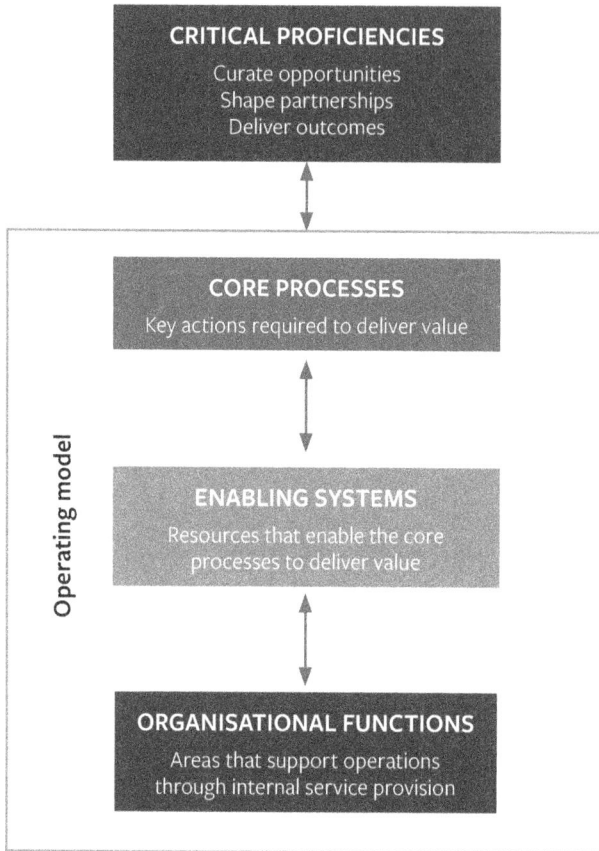

FIGURE 21: COMPONENTS OF AN OPERATING MODEL

We next start to assemble an operating model for universities, turning first to the alignment of core processes with the critical proficiencies, then to some of the associated enabling systems before briefly touching on various organisational functions (with which readers will be familiar).

HOW CORE PROCESSES FIT IN

An operating model capable of deriving impact from a university should, in essence, involve several interconnected core processes as illustrated in Figure 22 and elaborated upon below.

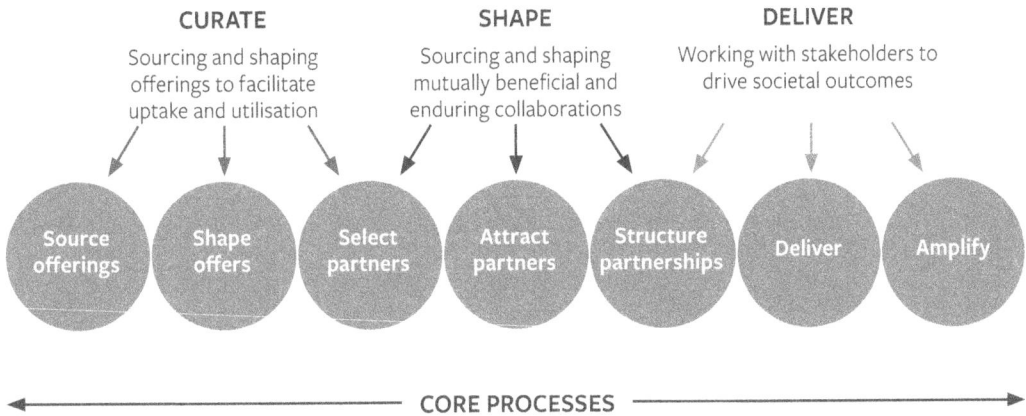

CURATE
Sourcing and shaping offerings to facilitate uptake and utilisation

SHAPE
Sourcing and shaping mutually beneficial and enduring collaborations

DELIVER
Working with stakeholders to drive societal outcomes

Source offerings

Shape offers

Select partners

Attract partners

Structure partnerships

Deliver

Amplify

◄──────── CORE PROCESSES ────────►

FIGURE 22: CORE PROCESSES

The curation of opportunities typically involves sourcing offerings, shaping potential offers, and identifying potential partners (a key component of selecting which partners to work with) that can help to address a societal issue. Consistent with a university's organisational direction, a key objective is to ensure that tangible education programs, products or services are utilised by as many people in need as possible. And, as proposed earlier (Chapter 2, Spheres of Impact), partnerships are required to achieve this objective.

The shaping of partnerships typically involves determining which of the identified partners to target (based on opportunities and the overarching organisational direction); attracting those partners to opportunities and offerings; and structuring enduring partnerships capable of delivering the education programs, products or services to as many people in need as possible.

These actions then transition to delivering the education programs, products or services as agreed, working together with partners to deliver intended outcomes, and scaling collaborations to ensure that as many people in need as possible receive the associated benefits.

HOW ENABLING SYSTEMS FIT IN

Enabling systems that support the core processes are likely to differ from university to university, but most can be grouped into the major categories detailed in Figure 23.

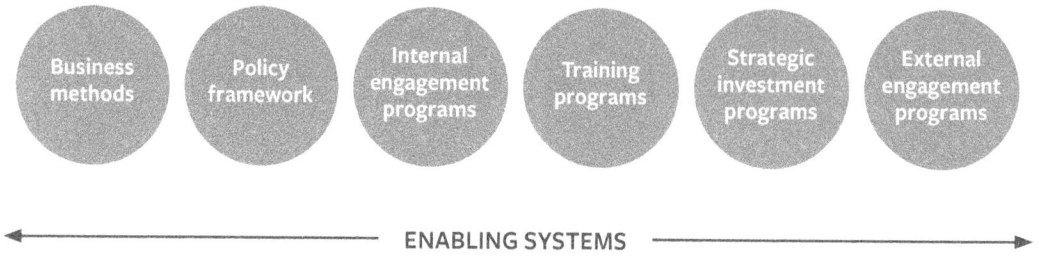

FIGURE 23: ENABLING SYSTEMS

Business methods

Business methods help university staff undertake their various roles and meet their university's objectives, and are therefore critical to success. Business methods are often fit-for-purpose and proprietary. They can add a competitive advantage by bringing together strategy, people and roles, structures and responsibilities, systems, and procedures.

Typically, universities develop operating procedures that support their core processes. Some key areas include strategic and operation planning, human resource management, workplace health and safety, administration and records, budget management and finance, reporting, office facilities, workflow planning, and approval processes and other protocols (e.g. ministerial visits and events).

They also develop methods and guidelines to facilitate the undertaking of the core processes, and support staff in undertaking their various roles. Some key areas include best-practice approaches for consultancy and commercial research engagements, material transfer, disclosure and assessment of intellectual property, protection of IP, commercialisation, new venture establishment, and creation and operations of internal units (or enterprises).

Policy framework

A policy framework is required to enable supportive activities to occur across complex organisational structures. The policy framework must signal intent. It incentivises and rewards staff for the achievement of organisational direction, establishes governance (including risk mitigation), directs procedures (including approvals for resource allocation and partnering), and establishes expected conduct. Policies can be diverse, but when framed with organisational direction they are critical to galvanising aligned activities.

Internal engagement programs

Building internal relationships and awareness of capabilities across an organisation, and the resultant exploration of opportunities that includes the full gamut of underlying assets and potential partners, is driven by purposeful internal-engagement activities, utilising various internal-engagement channels (as explored in Chapter 6).

Training programs

Supplementing internal-engagement activities, and with a view to driving next-generation derivation of impact, are various training programs in the form of internal-education workshops and seminars. These are integral to encouraging participation, and equipping staff with the skills to curate opportunities, shape partnerships and deliver outcomes. Many leading programs run by universities provide hands-on experience at the same time as curating opportunities.

Strategic investment

Strategic investment is often required by universities to advance various innovations or opportunities to a stage where they are ready to be advanced with partners. This involves a professional application, evaluation and approval process for investment, followed by active monitoring and business development, with a view to advancing to a partnership. Many universities introduce specialist proof-of-concept and early-stage investment capability, and innovative funding models to support the curation of opportunities.

External engagement programs (outreach)

The building of relationships with external organisations, including awareness of their capabilities, is crucial to the exploration of holistic solutions to societal challenges with potential partners, and this is achieved through purposeful external-engagement activities utilising various external channels (as explored in Chapter 6).

Examples of Enabling Systems Supporting Core Processes

Some examples of the types of enabling systems that support the core processes required to derive impact from universities are detailed in the following pages.

Integral to each core process is the engagement model, those necessary internal- and external-engagement activities that operate in tandem.

Core Process	Enabling Systems (Examples Only)	Purposes (Examples Only)
Source Offerings	Internal and external engagement	Enlist opportunities, orient and activate internal resources, understand problems / challenges.
	Databases, networks and market research	Examine societal and market need, trends, market segments sizes and growth, industry structures, and competitive environments.
	Education workshops and seminars	Increase awareness, encourage participation and explore opportunities.
	Concept generation workshops	Elicit ideas, utilise expert knowledge, and formulate opportunities.
	Tender alert systems	Consider problems articulated by external organisations and seek possible solutions.
	Idea capture and registration	Record ideas, inventions and concepts for assessment and potential progression.
Shape Offers	Internal and external engagement	Articulate nature of problems, assess underlying assets, and craft potential solutions, partnership models, and value propositions.
	Proposal preparation / tender responses	Articulate problem, potential solution, value proposition and proposed terms.
	Commercial assessments	Protect IP and facilitation of commercial uptake.
	Strategic investment	Advance innovations to viable programs, products or services for uptake.

Core Process	Enabling Systems (Examples Only)	Purposes (Examples Only)
Identify / Decide Partners	Internal and external engagement	Identify existing or potential partners that provide a viable pathway to market and have the desired capabilities.
	Databases, networks and market research	Explore existing or potential partners that may provide a pathway to market and assess suitability and capabilities.
	Industry body memberships	Leverage networks, glean industry structures and determine viable partners.
	Due diligence	Select reputable partners that can deliver required outcomes.
Attract Partners	Internal and external engagement	Utilise internal and external networks to attract identified suitable partners.
	Proposal preparation and responses to tenders	Articulate solution to problem along with value proposition and terms.
	Strategic partner and outreach programs	Determine needs and requirements and explore solutions that can be delivered in partnership.
Structure Partnerships	Internal and external engagement	Craft acceptable deal structures and associated terms and conditions.
	Commercial expertise and systems	Develop novel, flexible, fit-for-purpose deal structures, and streamlining processes.
	Policy and governance frameworks	Manage partnerships, deal structures, risk management and approval processes.
Deliver	Internal and external engagement	Actively manage partnership scope, requirements and deliverables.
	Project leadership and management	Ensure partnerships deliver as promised, enhance uptake and utilisation by people in need.
	Customer relationship management	Establish longer term relationships, repeat assistance and other solutions to problems.
Amplify	Internal and external engagement	Explore best practice, conceptualise new models, pilot new programs, implement new solutions, measure effectiveness.
	Stakeholder relationship management.	Expand spheres of influence to address societal issues in collaboration with multiple stakeholders.

For large and diverse universities with complex organisational structures, the engagement model and operating model must function together. When shaped around the critical proficiencies required to successfully derive impact, they complement each other.

ORGANISATIONAL FUNCTIONS

Organisational functions involve the many areas of an organisation that provide professional services internally. They are likely to be very diverse from university to university, but most can be grouped into the following broad, recognisable categories.

ORGANISATIONAL FUNCTIONS

FIGURE 24: ORGANISATIONAL FUNCTIONS

All universities will have some variant of the organisational functions detailed in Figure 24. It is beyond the remit of this book to delve into all the organisational functions of universities. However, a few matters pertinent to deriving impact from universities should be noted.

First, the allocation of resources from each organisational function is best coordinated through a common understanding across the university business of critical proficiencies and core processes. This enables resources to be directed towards the achievement of organisational direction. Ensuring that this understanding occurs across the full spectrum of organisational functions requires purposeful engagement coupled with purposeful activities that are brought together by an effective implementation model (see Chapter 8, Implementation Model).

Second, universities are a 'people' business, and each organisational function comprises people. Many roles are highly specialised, and it takes many different aptitudes, skills and experiences to operate a university effectively. The operating model demonstrates how and why the attraction, development, motivation, deployment, management and satisfaction of high-calibre staff are core elements of a university's successes.

Further, team structures and the ways that people work together are clearly critical to success, and this applies to specialist groups within universities that support the teaching, learning and research agendas. Good people can make organisational functions work if they are aligned with a university's organisational direction, and they keep the associated critical proficiencies at the core of what they do. These aspects also reflect the importance of the third aspect of developing organisational character: the implementation model.

Third, undertakings associated with deriving impact fundamentally involve managing relationships and therefore involve strategic conversations between stakeholders. These conversations are the two-way exchanges (speaking and listening) that must occur both internally and externally (consistent with purposeful engagement) to marshal stakeholders and align activities.

Strategic conversations should not be confused with communications. The management of these conversations is a pivotal leadership task and integral to an implementation model. By contrast, communications support strategic conversations through, for example, the promulgation of offerings to attract partners, requirements to get things done, and outcomes to celebrate successes and build brand and reputation.

Fourth, an operating model (including its enabling programs and organisational functions) involves elements of management, monitoring and control, and includes the measuring of performance.[1] Additionally, the benefits to society of the utilisation of programs or products, or the receiving of services sourced from universities, must be calculated to provide a true measure of the value that universities contribute to society.[2]

ESTABLISHING AN OPERATING MODEL

An operating model that supports a university's organisational direction, and which is designed around the critical proficiencies, enhances the likelihood of deriving impact. The fundamental components of an operating model for a university are summarised in Figure 25.

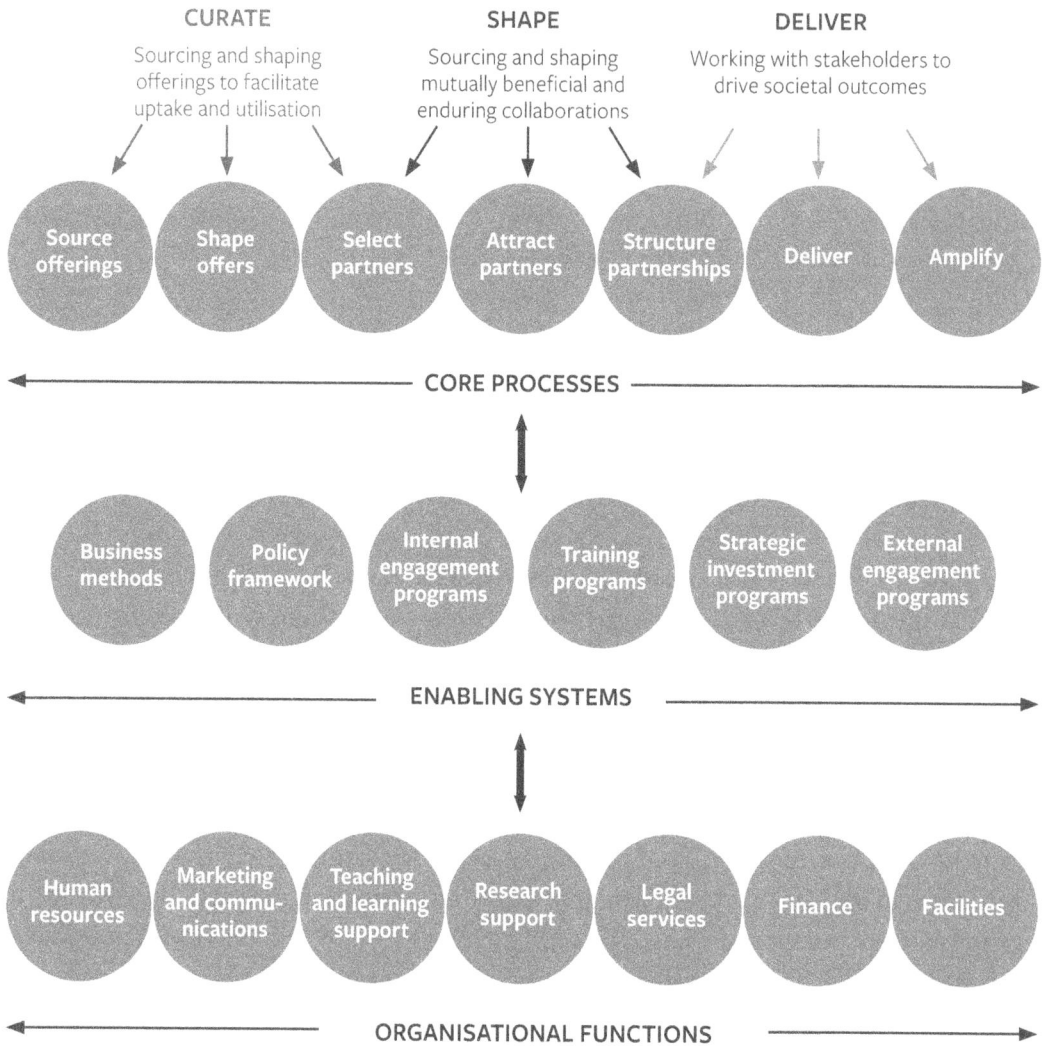

CURATE	SHAPE	DELIVER
Sourcing and shaping offerings to facilitate uptake and utilisation	Sourcing and shaping mutually beneficial and enduring collaborations	Working with stakeholders to drive societal outcomes

Source offerings · Shape offers · Select partners · Attract partners · Structure partnerships · Deliver · Amplify

CORE PROCESSES

Business methods · Policy framework · Internal engagement programs · Training programs · Strategic investment programs · External engagement programs

ENABLING SYSTEMS

Human resources · Marketing and communications · Teaching and learning support · Research support · Legal services · Finance · Facilities

ORGANISATIONAL FUNCTIONS

FIGURE 25: ESTABLISHING AN OPERATING MODEL

Continually asking the following questions helps universities design and establish an operating model capable of deriving impact:

Question 1: What core processes help deliver value?
Question 2: What enabling systems provide supporting activities and programs?
Question 3: What professional services are required to support core processes and enabling systems?

There are many universities that understand their environments, have a lock on important resources, employ finely tuned service-delivery processes, and work hard at relationships with stakeholders; however, if these activities occur in isolation, universities still struggle to derive impact.

This brings us to the third aspect of organisational character required to deliver organisational direction in today's ever-changing environments: the implementation model, the aspect required to pull all elements into a cohesive whole.

Chapter 7 Endnotes

1.   Traditionally, performance can be monitored utilising *market*-performance or *financial*-performance measures. Market-performance measures, such as student enrolments, research grants, publications, partnerships, student or partner attitudes and loyalty, and the changes in these over time, can be related to the original objectives of the organisational direction being pursued. Financial performance is typically measured through a monitoring of revenue or funding contributions, relative to the resources employed to achieve them. Both market and financial measures typically include qualitative and quantitative metrics. To be most effective, performance measures should also include factors other than those used to set objectives to ensure that the wider implications have not been lost in the pursuit of those objectives.

2.   Perhaps because of the difficulty with estimations and measurement, the benefits to society from the utilisation of programs, products or receiving services sourced from universities is less prevalent. But it is here that the true value of universities to society manifests, and universities, together with key stakeholders, need to advance an understanding of methodologies to assess this value creation. Further, universities are significant financial and social institutions. They have profound direct impacts on a region and the broader economy. For example, direct impacts on a region can come from university and student income and expenditure, R&D contributions, skills development and retention, provision of infrastructure, voluntary activities, and community service and cultural opportunities. From this there are multiplier effects on output, income and employment; fiscal effects (such as increased tax revenues); and community benefits such as security, diversity, community development and social cohesion. Universities contribute to the development of regional industry through critical mass, new collaborations and partnerships, and upskilling of workforces. Here, too, the advancement of methodologies to assess this value creation is required.

IMPLEMENTATION MODEL

'I can't change the direction of the wind, but I can adjust my sails to always reach my destination.'

—Jimmy Dean, country music artist

KEY THEMES

- Understanding the nature of decisions and activities that support decision-making

- Framing system-based activities around the nature of decisions

- Understanding how decision-making anchors, operating contexts and forms of engagement inform decisions

- Harmonisation of activities through strategic conversations and values and behaviours

The vision of top universities goes beyond the immediate impact of the solutions they provide. They also observe the unique perspectives that universities bring to different social situations. These valuable perspectives are the offspring of its people. With sophisticated powers of perception, a university maintains the capacity to influence and redefine key sectors of society while also understanding and addressing the needs and demands of students, partners, entrepreneurs, business leaders, government, and the broader community. The quality of this effort can set a university apart when it comes to deriving impact, and it is conspicuous among university leaders who sense change, learn from change and adjust accordingly when making decisions in the face of uncertainty. An effective implementation model makes this consistently possible by fusing the required organisational direction and organisational character into a cohesive framework.

In this chapter, we assemble an implementation-model framework for a university incorporating the contexts and landscapes that influence leaders' decisions. Purposeful engagement and a complex of system-based activities are also built into this matrix, whose ultimate focus must settle on those who will be the implementers: the people of a university.

THE NATURE OF DECISIONS

University leaders must know and understand the operating landscape in which the institution is located, and how this environment influences the process of decision-making. They must be focused and clear-minded, and their decisions involving strategy and its implementation must weigh up highly influential external and internal factors. Mapping the nature of these decisions and what shapes them represents ground zero for the development of a framework for an implementation model. To commence this mapping process, our attention falls first on strategic decisions.

Strategic decisions (and operating landscape)

For an organisation like a university, strategic decisions involve answering questions raised in earlier chapters such as:

- Whom do we serve?
- What is our ambition, value, and purpose?
- What distinguishes us?

- What market segments should we target?
- What paths to market should we pursue?
- What competitive value propositions should we offer?
- What underlying assets do we need so our offerings are better than the alternatives?

In responding to these questions, strategic decision-making is influenced by both external and internal environments (collectively described as the 'operating landscape'). External factors that can influence strategic decisions include demographic trends, size of markets and their growth rates, competition, industry structures, economic conditions, geopolitical climate, and exterior factors (such as weather events or pandemics).

Internal factors that can influence strategic decisions generally comprise a university's underlying assets. Typically, these include knowledge (e.g. education programs, research outcomes and publications), research capabilities (e.g. expertise, specialist equipment, facilities and research methodology), innovations (e.g. technologies and associated rights), financial position, enabling systems and organisational functions. The predominant factor in this context is arguably the people of a university, and the quality of their relationships and interactions.

Implementation decisions (and operating context)

Implementation decisions are also foundational here. These require answers to questions such as:

- What are the facts and how should we respond?
- What are the options, and which should we choose?
- How do we garner the knowledge we need to make decisions, and what are our next critical steps?
- What is required and who should we involve?

These decisions need to be aligned with the strategic decisions that are heavily influenced by the operating landscapes (external and internal environments) that universities traverse. These landscapes can be broad and varied, and their numerous states of flux may be categorised at different moments in terms of three operating contexts, namely (1) defined, (2) complicated, and (3) complex. In a defined operating context, matters are relatively predictable due to relatively static environments. A complicated operating context is less predictable and involves variability in outcomes. A complex environment involves uncertainty and dynamism, and is relatively unpredictable.

The context in which a university operates at any given moment has a major bearing on the nature of information gathering and the required approaches to decision-making and implementation.

With this perspective, we can now set in place the first layer of a framework to shape and inform an implementation model. The matrix presented in Figure 26 establishes four realms, demonstrating how a university's operating landscape influences strategic decisions (spanning realms one and two); and how operating context, as a function of operating landscape, influences implementation decisions (spanning realms three and four).

Nature of Decisions

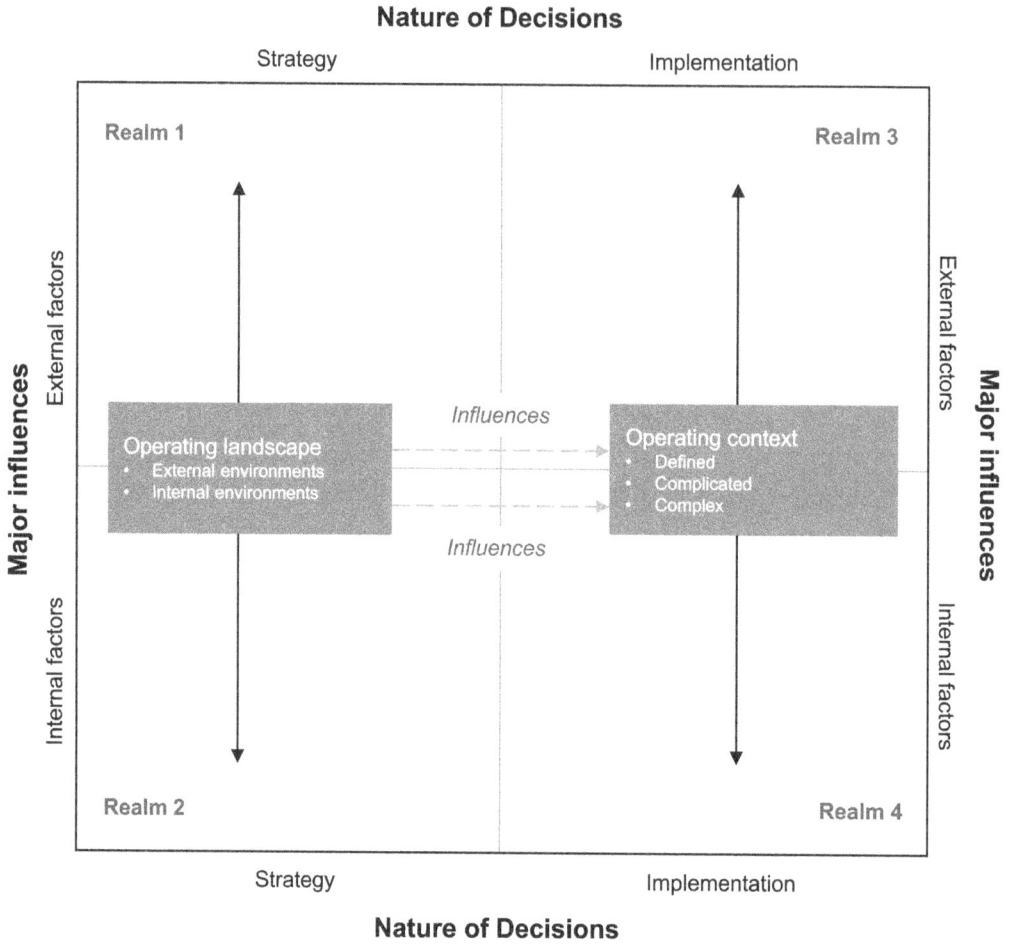

FIGURE 26: NATURE OF DECISIONS AND MAJOR INFLUENCES

Any organisation needs to determine how strategic decisions and implementation decisions are brought synergistically together to yield success. Therefore, we now turn to those factors that are key in doing so—the 'anchors' for all decision making.

ANCHORING ALL DECISION-MAKING

Earlier chapters presented three concepts critical to deriving impact from universities. *Intent*, a combination of direction and purpose, is predominantly influenced by external factors. *Critical proficiencies*, those matters at which a university must excel to derive socio-economic impact, are at the heart of all matters. An *operating model*, the core processes, enabling systems and organisational functions to deliver value to stakeholders, is heavily influenced by internal factors.

These three concepts provide the anchors for decision-making. They are inherently interrelated and central to galvanising shared action. In the context of an implementation model, they can also be university bellwethers, spanning both strategic and implementation decisions. In this way they indicate to university leaders the broad trends that guide the decision-making that is intended to derive impact. Returning to the matrix mentioned earlier, these anchors can now be mapped as depicted in Figure 27.

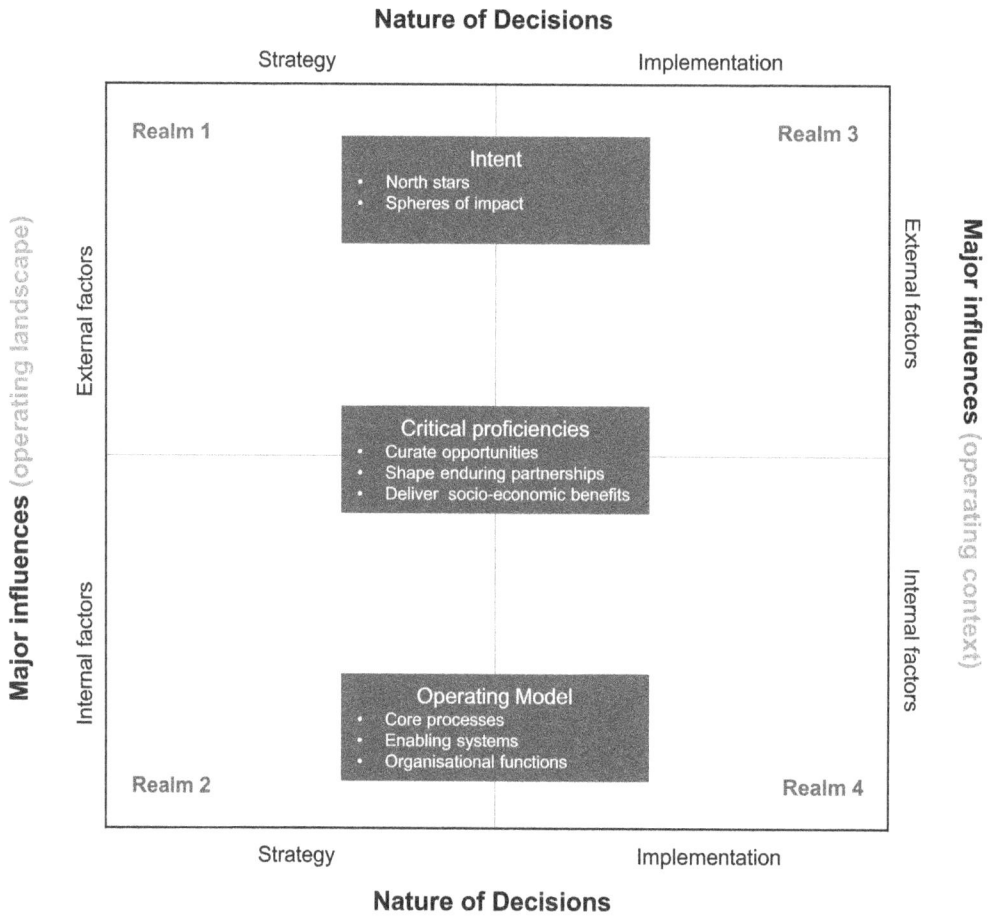

FIGURE 27: ANCHORING ALL DECISION-MAKING

The matrix illustrates that all realms are brought together through a focus on the critical proficiencies (and are therefore central to all decision-making). It shows how strategic and implementation decisions, which are predominantly influenced by external factors, are fused through the establishment of intent. Strategic and implementation decisions, which are predominantly influenced by internal factors, are galvanised through an operating model, with the core processes, enabling systems and organisational functions framed around intent and aligned to the critical proficiencies.

THE NATURE OF ACTIVITIES

With the anchors for decision-making, and the major influences on the same decision-making demonstrated above, we now move to the nature of activities used by universities to frame the information required for decision-making. We turn to the activities the university must undertake to nurture unique perspectives that help deliver great socio-economic benefits. To do this, it is contended that any organisation, including universities and their people, must undertake five system-based activities: sensing, sourcing, marshalling, serving, and harmonising, the most critical of the five.

In the case of *sensing*, a university must be aware of opportunities outside its confines, including any community issues that need to be resolved. An interactive exercise in sensing what is occurring must continually be undertaken by leaders and staff, always with reference to a university's underlying assets, which may be advantageous or fall short of what is required.

In the case of *sourcing*, a university must build or acquire key resources to capture such opportunities, resolve pressing issues, leverage advantages, and address shortcomings. This involves the ability to source assets such as talented people along with their associated knowledge, research capabilities, innovations, partnership potential, and financial capital.

In the case of *marshalling*, universities with multiple stakeholders must be able to obtain and impart the right information for decision-making, garner the right level of support and resources, and align all key stakeholders and endeavours toward the delivery of great socio-economic benefits. They must maintain mutually beneficial relationships and satisfy a wide range of stakeholders.

In the case of *serving*, universities must be able to assemble effective teams of people and create productive partnerships that serve the broad social agenda through their interactions in delivering socio-economic benefits.

Finally, universities need to make this system of activities function effectively. On a fundamental level, sourcing alone cannot achieve its intended impact in isolation from sensing. On a more complex level, the activities around sensing, sourcing, marshalling, and serving must be harmonised to ensure that people link insights and ideas; and draw together assets and resources, directing them toward meeting the needs and wants of their stakeholders. *Harmonising* is the process by which context is created for an organisation's people; it pulls all activities together, working towards a set of tangible outputs.

The importance of such interactions to a university's implementation model is evident, as is the need for the organisational structures that foster and nurture these activities. These activities enable a university to source the information needed efficiently when making decisions on university business and societal benefit. Therefore, this system-based view is extrapolated onto the implementation model using the model framework in Figure 28.

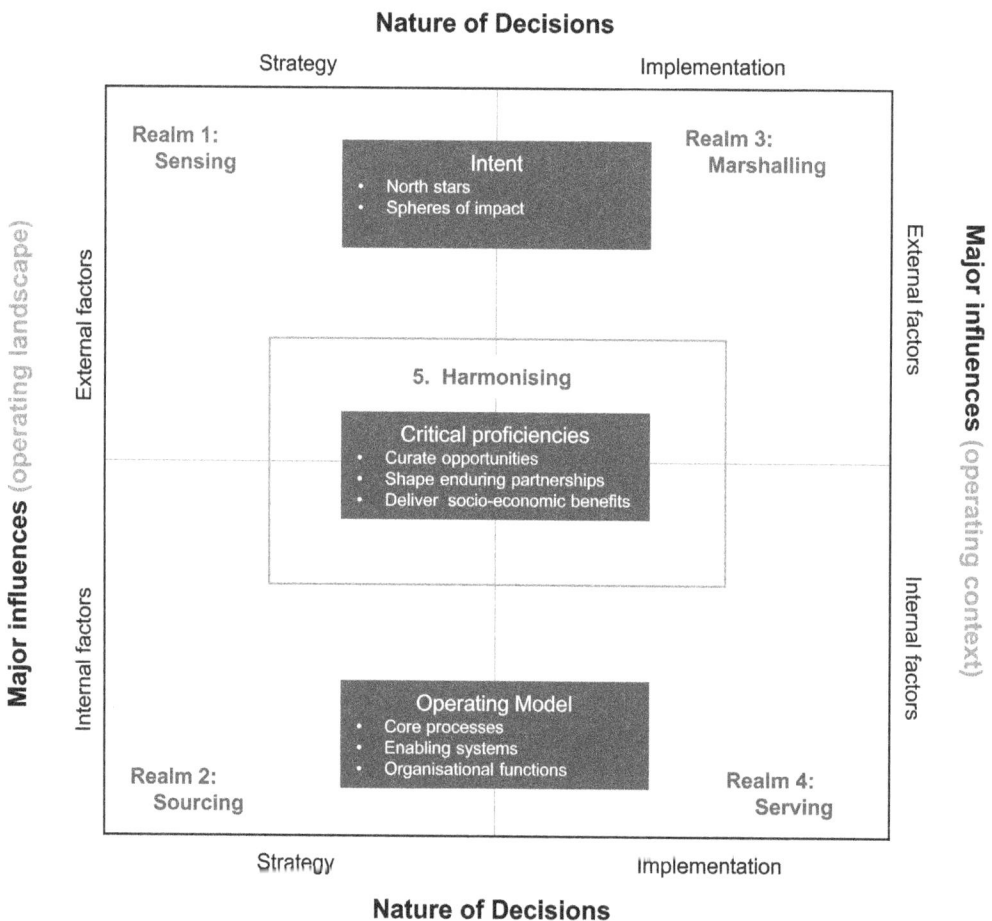

Nature of Decisions

Strategy   Implementation

Realm 1: Sensing   Realm 3: Marshalling

Major influences (operating landscape)

External factors   Internal factors

Intent
- North stars
- Spheres of impact

5. Harmonising

Critical proficiencies
- Curate opportunities
- Shape enduring partnerships
- Deliver socio-economic benefits

Operating Model
- Core processes
- Enabling systems
- Organisational functions

Realm 2: Sourcing   Realm 4: Serving

Major influences (operating context)

External factors   Internal factors

Strategy   Implementation

Nature of Decisions

FIGURE 28: SYSTEM-BASED ACTIVITIES AND DECISION-MAKING

Realm one of the implementation-model framework, involving strategic decisions heavily influenced by external factors, is the domain of sensing. Realm two, involving strategic decisions heavily influenced by internal factors, is the domain of sourcing. Realm three, involving implementation decisions heavily influenced by external factors, is the domain of marshalling. And realm four, involving implementation decisions heavily influenced by internal factors, is the domain of serving. Harmonisation of activities spans all realms; it encompasses synergistically coordinating sensing, sourcing, marshalling and serving.

These concepts are introduced here with the injection of system-based activities into the framework being assembled. They will be revisited in more detail later in this chapter. First, however, our attention turns to how decision-making is approached, and the right approach is ensured.

IDENTIFYING APPROACHES TO DECISIONS

Each university will take a different approach to a major strategic or significant implementation decision; however, by focusing on each decision-making realm and its associated system-based activity, some key approaches can be revealed. Two approaches in the realms of strategic decisions (realm one and realm two) have been explored in Part I of this book (Organisational Direction). The first involves discerning the opportunity spectrum (realm one) and the need to position and prioritise competitively. The second involves understanding the knowledge-capital value chain (realm two) so that a core strategy can be developed, and associated resourcing decisions made.

Two additional approaches in the realms of implementation decisions (realm three and realm four) are introduced later in this chapter. The first involves determining the required leadership foci and decision-making frameworks (realm three), considering how to decide on the focus of leadership, the ways information is obtained and imparted, and how decisions are best made. Heavily influencing these factors is the operating context associated with the various opportunities a university chooses to pursue.

The second additional approach (realm four) is concerned with how people and teams are arranged to ensure that opportunities are taken, and decisions implemented effectively. In essence, this is about matching the right skills, experience and attributes to the tasks at hand. This approach recognises both the distinction between position (a function of staff) and role (required task), and the importance of this distinction when allocating staff to the various key actions (or core processes) required to deliver socio-economic benefits. These implementation decisions are heavily influenced by internal factors, but undertaken in light of the required leadership foci and decision-making frameworks.

By mapping each of the four approaches onto the framework, it can be demonstrated that each realm and associated system-based activity combines two aspects that anchor all decision-making for universities seeking to derive impact. Each realm also utilises a particular approach in the same instance, as illustrated in Figure 29.

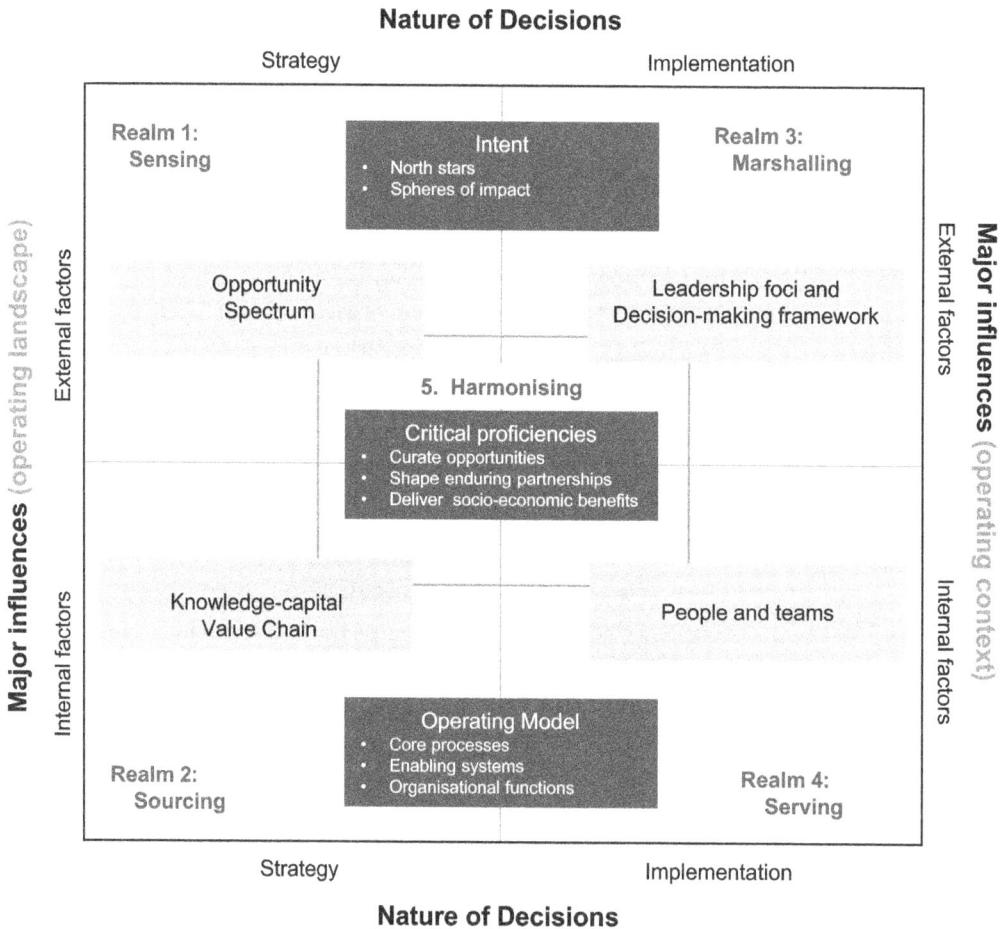

Nature of Decisions

	Strategy		Implementation	
Realm 1: Sensing		**Intent** • North stars • Spheres of impact		**Realm 3: Marshalling**
	Opportunity Spectrum		Leadership foci and Decision-making framework	
		5. Harmonising		
		Critical proficiencies • Curate opportunities • Shape enduring partnerships • Deliver socio-economic benefits		
	Knowledge-capital Value Chain		People and teams	
Realm 2: Sourcing		**Operating Model** • Core processes • Enabling systems • Organisational functions		**Realm 4: Serving**
	Strategy		Implementation	

Major influences (operating landscape) — External factors / Internal factors (left)

Major influences (operating context) — External factors / Internal factors (right)

Nature of Decisions

FIGURE 29: APPROACHES TO MAKE DECISIONS

For example, realm one of the implementation-model framework involves making strategic decisions through sensing. Activities associated with sensing are anchored by intent and critical proficiencies, and utilise the opportunity spectrum as an approach to competitively position and prioritise opportunities that can derive impact.

The interplay between system-based activities, decision-making anchors and approaches for each decision-making realm are explored in more detail later in this chapter. First, we turn to the importance of purposeful engagement for an implementation model.

OBTAINING AND IMPARTING INFORMATION

The need to obtain and impart the information necessary for both strategic and implementation decisions has guided the construction of this implementation-model framework from the outset. The process of accumulating useful knowledge is undertaken in a university through purposeful engagement. These are internal and external engagement activities that operate in tandem, and are aligned with each critical component of deriving impact (Chapter 6, Engagement Model).

Purposeful engagement should be embarked upon with clear objectives, for example (1) setting organisational direction, (2) curating opportunities, (3) shaping enduring partnerships, and (4) delivering outcomes. Clarity of objective helps determine the purpose of engaging, which in turn frames the questions to be answered and sharpens the focus of engagement activities required to answer them.

Approaching engagement purposefully is an important step away from arbitrary and reactionary activities and towards the focused system-based activities required to derive impact. Purposeful engagement (to obtain and impart information) and system-based activities (to decide and drive outcomes) are intertwined. Bringing them together requires the right conversations and actions at the right time involving the right people: the process of harmonisation. In moments of system-based activity, the repertoire of knowledge, expertise, information and skills garnered through purposeful engagement is put to work in the deliberate interactions of people who want to get the job done.

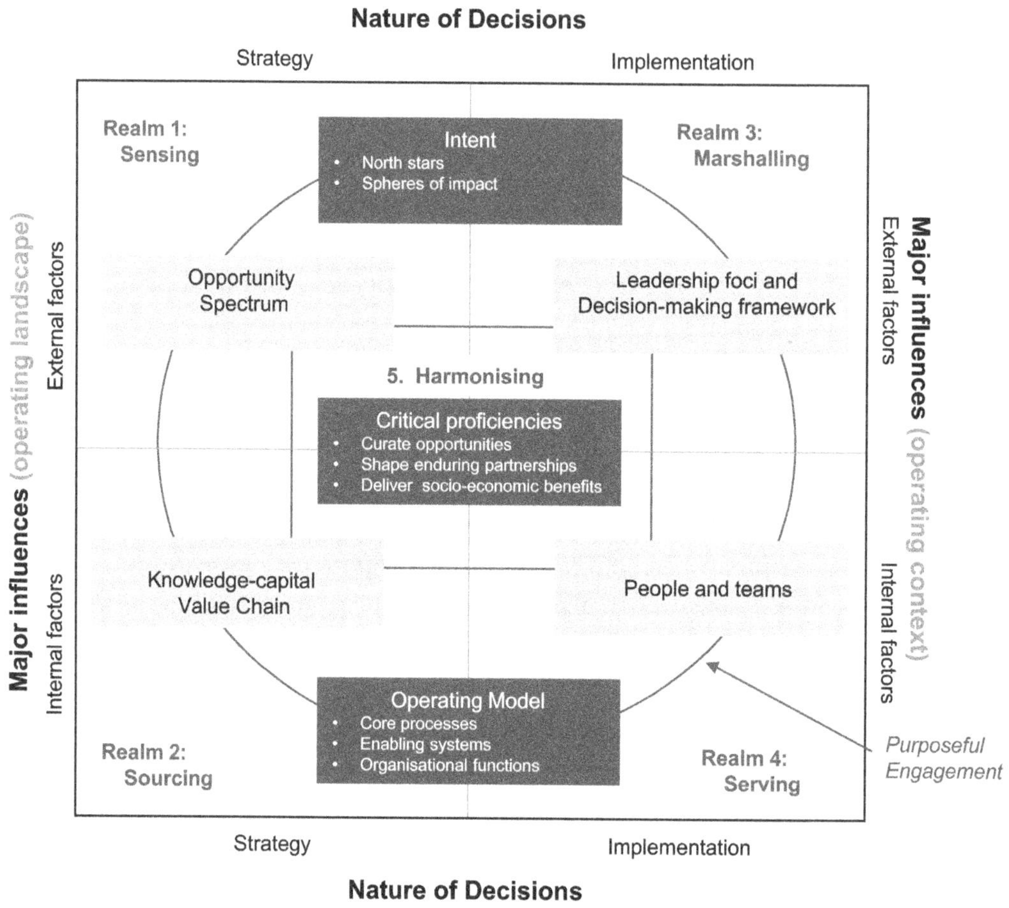

Nature of Decisions

Strategy · Implementation

Realm 1: Sensing

Realm 3: Marshalling

Intent
- North stars
- Spheres of impact

Opportunity Spectrum

Leadership foci and Decision-making framework

5. Harmonising

Critical proficiencies
- Curate opportunities
- Shape enduring partnerships
- Deliver socio-economic benefits

Knowledge-capital Value Chain

People and teams

Operating Model
- Core processes
- Enabling systems
- Organisational functions

Realm 2: Sourcing

Realm 4: Serving

Purposeful Engagement

Strategy · Implementation

Nature of Decisions

Major influences (operating landscape) — External factors — Internal factors

Major influences (operating context) — External factors — Internal factors

FIGURE 30: OBTAINING AND IMPARTING INFORMATION

The activities of university people are explored in further depth next, when the concepts of sensing, sourcing, marshalling, serving, and harmonisation are brought to life.

STRATEGY-ORIENTED ACTIVITIES

We start with the two system-based activities required to continually develop strategies that help navigate rapidly changing and challenging environments: sensing and sourcing.

Sensing (realm one)

Sensing predominantly involves establishing intent, discerning a university's opportunity spectrum, and making strategic decisions based on these. Importantly, these undertakings must be constant and continual, enabling the university to make strategic decisions that position it consistently and competitively. This endeavour is heavily influenced by external factors, including market attractiveness, industry structure and competition, and a suitable position must be ascertained relative to a university's underlying assets and potential offerings.

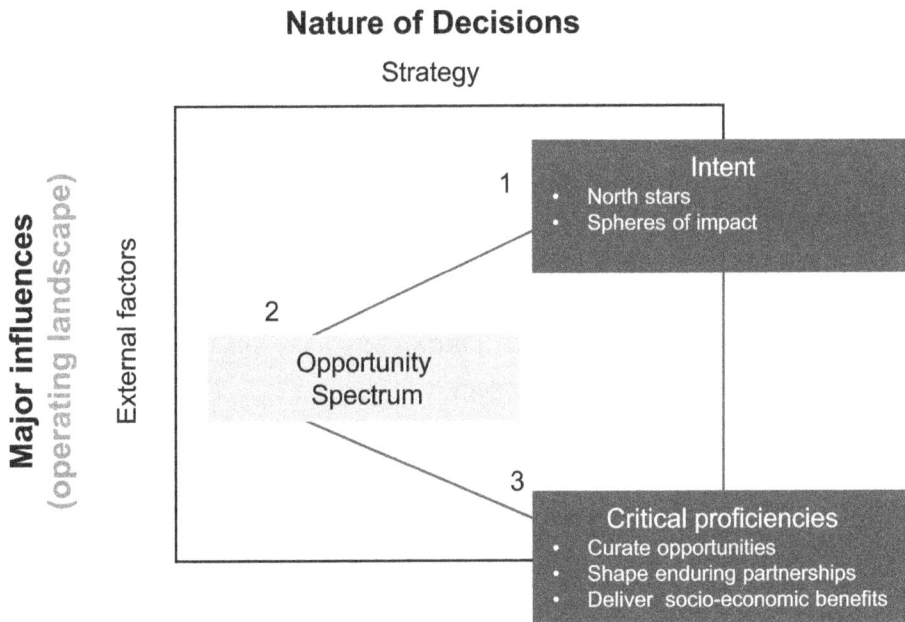

FIGURE 31: SENSING (REALM 1)

Purposeful engagement for decision-making involves informing decisions. Internal engagement is focused on examining underlying assets, organisational alignment, delivery mechanisms, and competitive strengths. External engagement is focused on seeking major demographic shifts, societal needs, attractive markets, and paths-to-markets.

Here, purposeful activities of university staff must involve actions focused on (1) direction and purpose (north stars and spheres of impact) to establish and impart the university's intent, and (2) positioning competitively, matching consumer needs to competitive strengths (positioning) where university people decide which opportunities to pursue and in what order (prioritising). These combine to form the opportunity spectrum. And, as with all the identified system-based activities, each associated purposeful activity must focus on (3) the critical proficiencies: the curation of opportunities; shaping of enduring partnerships, and delivery of socio-economic benefits; in other words, the *how* questions.

Sourcing (realm two)

Sourcing is enabled and obligated by an understanding of the knowledge-capital value chain. Specifically, these are the strategic decisions necessary to ascertain needs, build matching value propositions, and arrange flexible, fit-for-purpose approaches to maximise impact. This endeavour is heavily influenced by internal factors (including the nature of underlying assets and associated delivery mechanisms), but decisions are also made with reference to differing markets and paths-to-markets, and therefore a university's opportunity spectrum.

Nature of Decisions

Strategy

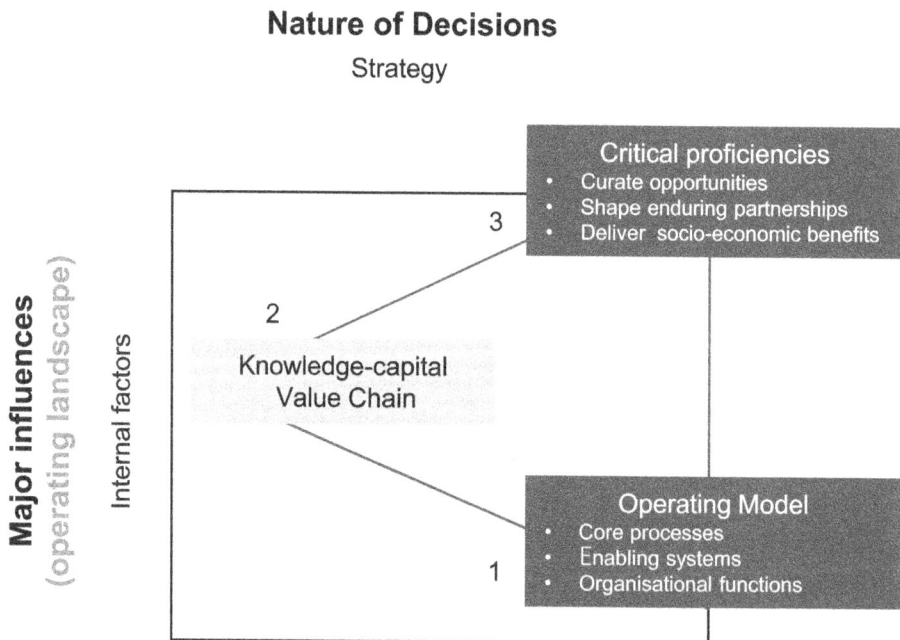

FIGURE 32: SOURCING (REALM 2)

Purposeful engagement for decision-making involves (a) enlisting opportunities, with internal engagement focused on activating potential solutions, and external engagement focused on understanding needs and the nature of the problems to solve; and (b) structuring partnerships, with internal engagement focused on crafting enduring partnerships, and external engagement focused on attracting the right partners.

Here, purposeful activities of university staff must be focused on (1) operating model (see Figure 32), which includes the key actions required to deliver value (core processes), resources that enable the core processes to deliver value (enabling systems), and areas that support operations through internal service provision (organisational functions); (2) understanding the knowledge-capital value chain, which includes determining the nature of underlying assets, market segments, delivery mechanisms, and types of engagements; and (3) the critical proficiencies.

The interplay between sensing and sourcing

Strategic decisions involve detailed, creative and continual assessment of a university's capabilities relative to those of other providers, and of opportunities and threats posed by the external environment. Accordingly, the activities of sensing and sourcing are intertwined. These activities must also be continual since the opportunities and threats posed by the external environment, and the strengths and weaknesses of the internal environment, change continually.

On another level, target market segments must be identified and selected, and also competitive offerings defined and developed. Once again, the activities of sensing and sourcing work together to position a university and its offerings continually and competitively.

The garnering and imparting of information to support associated decisions and activities is undertaken through purposeful engagement utilising various engagement channels. The effects of this interplay are tangible education programs and research outcomes, and partnerships that can deliver programs, products or services to the community, and by so doing deliver great socio-economic benefits.

Of course, universities must also be able to put strategy into practice, and implementation decisions are therefore just as critical.

Strategic Decisions

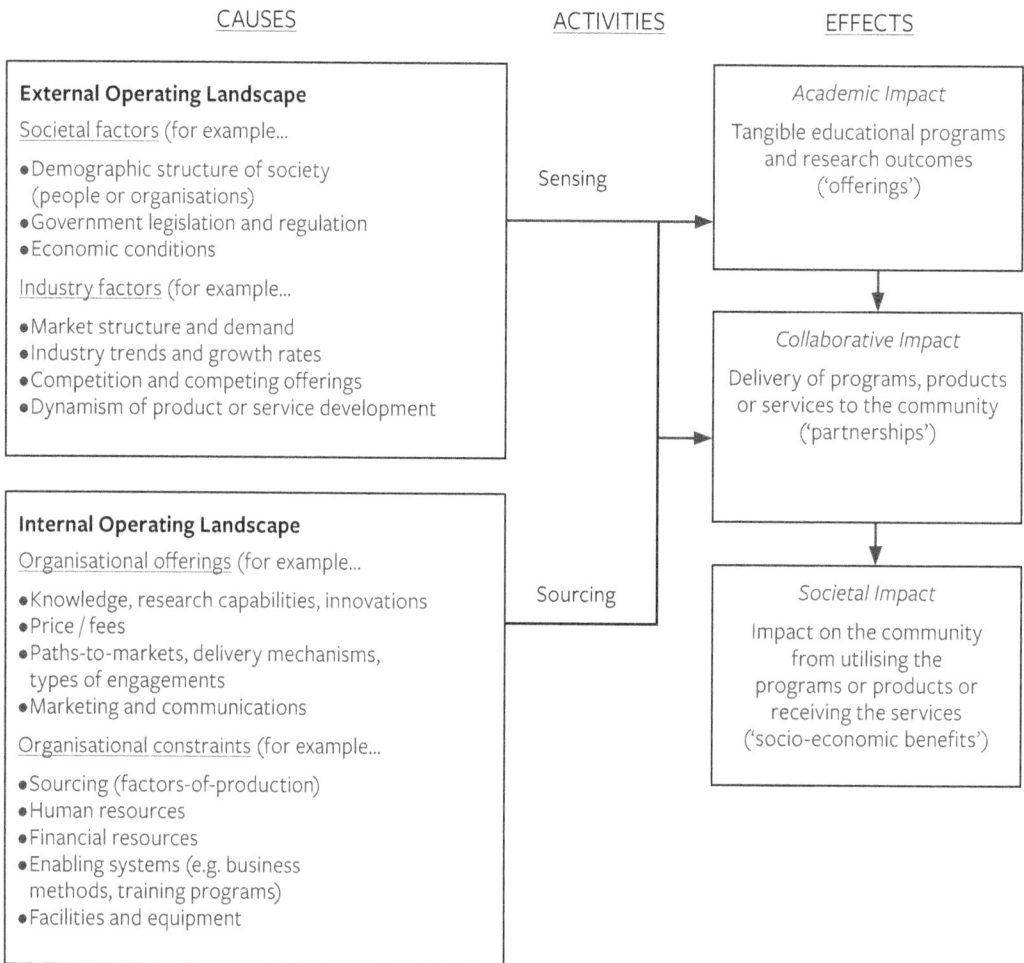

CAUSES   ACTIVITIES   EFFECTS

External Operating Landscape

Societal factors (for example...

- Demographic structure of society (people or organisations)
- Government legislation and regulation
- Economic conditions

Industry factors (for example...

- Market structure and demand
- Industry trends and growth rates
- Competition and competing offerings
- Dynamism of product or service development

Sensing

Academic Impact

Tangible educational programs and research outcomes ('offerings')

Collaborative Impact

Delivery of programs, products or services to the community ('partnerships')

Internal Operating Landscape

Organisational offerings (for example...

- Knowledge, research capabilities, innovations
- Price / fees
- Paths-to-markets, delivery mechanisms, types of engagements
- Marketing and communications

Organisational constraints (for example...

- Sourcing (factors-of-production)
- Human resources
- Financial resources
- Enabling systems (e.g. business methods, training programs)
- Facilities and equipment

Sourcing

Societal Impact

Impact on the community from utilising the programs or products or receiving the services ('socio-economic benefits')

FIGURE 33: THE INTERPLAY BETWEEN SENSING AND SOURCING

IMPLEMENTATION-ORIENTED ACTIVITIES

We now turn to the two system-based activities that are required to continually implement strategies and help traverse rapidly changing and challenging environments: marshalling and serving.

Marshalling (realm three)

Marshalling involves understanding the context in which a university operates, and allows a university to inform its leadership and decision-making processes. This can be the source of major competitive advantage in times of rapid change. The appropriate leadership foci and decision-making frameworks, and the related decisions on implementation, are dependent on the operating context at play and are heavily influenced by external factors.

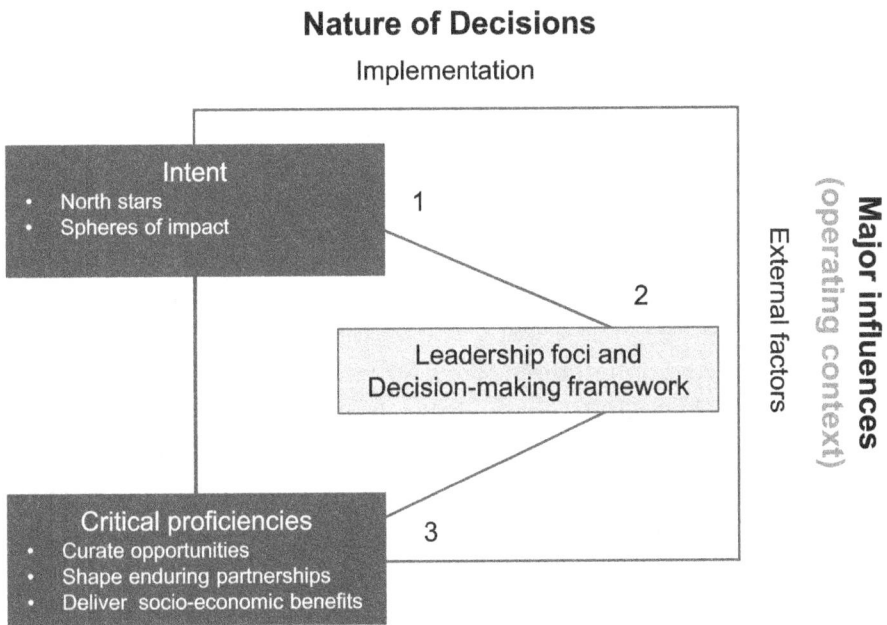

FIGURE 34: MARSHALLING (REALM 3)

Purposeful engagement for decision-making involves performance, with internal engagement focused on leading and managing to desired outcomes, and external engagement focused on amplifying the optimal partnerships.

Here, purposeful activities of university staff must be focused on (1) direction and purpose in order to action and impart a university's intent; (2) the operating context in order to realise the foci of leadership, and choose and implement the associated decision-making frameworks; and (3) the critical proficiencies.

Most importantly, because universities have a diversity of functions and operate across an array of environments, leadership focus and decision-making cannot be a one-size-fits-all proposition. Approaches to leadership and decision-making must change depending on the operating context that is faced.

This requirement for versatility and nimbleness of approach is explored now in relation to three operating contexts that universities currently face: (1) a defined operating context involving certain, static and therefore relatively predictable environments; (2) a complicated operating context involving changeable, active and therefore variable environments; and (3) a complex operating context involving uncertain, dynamic and relatively unpredictable environments.

Defined operating context: Leadership within universities is multifaceted but organisational direction, people, and operations tend to demand the most attention.

Within certain, static, and therefore relatively predictable environments, leadership typically focuses on (1) establishing clear objectives and goals to drive organisational direction; (2) ensuring staff are appropriately skilled and experienced; and (3) establishing appropriate policies, protocols, and processes to support operations. Until recently, most universities have been able to operate successfully in this way.

In a defined operating context, universities can operate in a routine fashion. Most matters are discernible, and processes exist to manage them. The enrolment of students, scheduling of lectures, lodging of grant applications (traditional to universities) involve highly defined (and refined) processes. The decision-making frameworks typically involve assessing the facts, classifying them and then responding accordingly. Perhaps because of the relatively predictable nature of this operating context, many of the associated processes are currently being automated, enabled by many of the digital platforms that now exist.

The administration of small-scale consulting or commercial research projects on standard terms of business provides an example of an approach to deriving impact that falls into a defined operating context. Staff need to be adept at identifying common factors, and reviewing contractual arrangements and responding appropriately. Managers and staff have access to necessary information for dealing with each situation, and directives tend to be straightforward, decisions easily delegated, and many functions automated.

In defined operating contexts you often see a major focus on key performance indicators, with emphasis on benchmarking against best practice. Many readers who operate in defined operating contexts will be quite familiar with these managerial approaches.

Complicated operating context: Our changing world is becoming increasingly unpredictable. Of necessity, universities are utilising broader leadership approaches and decision-making frameworks. With more potential options and ensuing actions arising, the focus of leadership must shift to (1) setting organisational direction and strategy (how universities position and obtain sustainable competitive advantage), (2) organisation and management of people to facilitate implementation of strategy, and (3) frameworks that support operations (concepts, information and principles). Most universities have shifted their emphasis toward this context since the turn of the millennium, particularly as traditional funding models are changing and competition is intensifying.

In a complicated operating context, there are typically matters that involve multiple options for universities, where judicious selection is required. In this operating context, the decision-making frameworks involve assessing information, analysing options and responding accordingly.

Articulating societal needs and root causes of challenges, shaping and assessing potential solutions, and selecting the best avenues and partners to maximise outcomes are approaches to deriving impact that fall into a complicated operating context. Here, there is a relationship between cause and effect, but making choices requires numerous staff with various levels of expertise and experience. Leaders must navigate expert opinions while stimulating ideas and creative solutions. Information is not always exhaustive or readily available, and judicious decisions need time.

There is much in the literature, particularly in the fields of strategy, management, marketing and general business on how to navigate complicated operating contexts, and it is beyond the scope of this book to address them all. One key aspect—the way in which people and teams are selected, assembled and operate—is critical in this operating context, and subsequently elaborated upon when canvassing the system-based activity of serving.

Complex operating context: A complex operating context involves navigating unpredictable and constantly changing circumstances. Much of contemporary business now faces aspects of this, particularly with new-business establishment (entrepreneurship) or business disruption (due to rapidly emerging alternatives or competition, or new ways to access customers and factors of production). New business opportunities or dynamic business environments require non-traditional planning cycles and approaches. 'Right' answers do not exist. Rather, information must be continually discovered and acted upon.

Universities are not exempt from this operating context, and those seeking to derive impact can also face inherently unpredictable or dynamic environments. This is often experienced with entrepreneurial endeavours, something that is becoming more of a priority for universities (see Chapter 1, North Stars) and with changes in the way knowledge, innovations and research capabilities are obtained by end-users (including students, organisations and the community).[1]

Uncertain and rapidly changing environments render many traditional leadership approaches ineffective. In these circumstances, leadership shifts focus to providing clear direction through well-articulated purpose; and shaping the context in which people can make up their own minds, apply their creativity, and make effective decisions. People must be empowered to do extraordinary things, but efforts must be aligned. Leadership must also focus on values that guide behaviour and on establishing a learning environment, where effective communication, feedback, and empowerment of staff, within the overarching purpose, are mission critical.

Decision-making frameworks in this context typically involve experimenting (in ways that yield useful knowledge and where it is relatively safe to fail),[2] and, based on information from that experimentation, assessing and responding accordingly. Continually obtaining knowledge to inform decisions and next steps is critical. Leaders must allow a path forward to be revealed and remain flexible as new information is obtained. It requires setting boundaries rather than making directives and allowing opportunities to evolve through continual actions. Open communication is essential to creating a learning environment. Key to success in complex operating contexts is the creation of an environment from which successful outcomes can emerge.

Directing leadership focus and decision-making frameworks: Through an understanding of the dimensions of the operating contexts in which they function (refer to Table 4), universities can guide leadership focus for organisational direction, people and operations, along with the application of associated decision-making frameworks when seeking to derive socio-economic benefits.

Dimensions of operating contexts

	DEFINED	COMPLICATED	COMPLEX
Nature of context	• Certain • Static • Predictable	• Changeable • Active • Variable	• Uncertain • Dynamic • Unpredictable
Leadership foci	• Objectives and goals • Skills • Processes	• Strategy • Management • Frameworks	• Orientation • Empowerment • Learnings
Decision-making framework	• Assess facts • Categorise tasks • Respond/administer	• Assess information • Analyse options • Select best course of action	• Experiment • Assess outcomes • Respond and refine/repeat
Examples	• Routine commercial research projects involving standard terms of business	• Large-scale, multi-party collaborations • Co-development of new products underpinned by innovations and associated IP rights	• New business opportunities, involving new to the world products and services • New business models

TABLE 4: LEADERSHIP FOCUS AND DECISION-MAKING FRAMEWORKS

Serving (realm four)

Serving is first and foremost about an important truth: a university is all about people. Universities aiming to derive impact can nominally position education programs within competitive environments and be seen to pursue research outcomes for society's betterment. However, any university's success in such ventures is due in large part to its people, and how they are brought together to collectively derive socio-economic benefits.

Nature of Decisions

Implementation

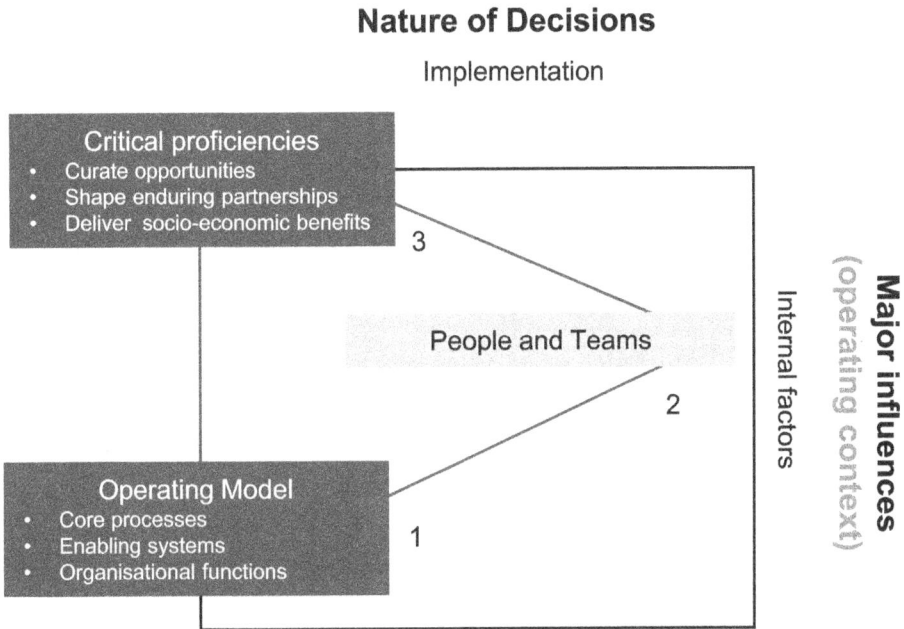

FIGURE 35: SERVING (REALM 4)

Purposeful engagement involves collaboration, with internal engagement focused on accountability, and external engagement with partners focused on common purpose.

To deliver socio-economic benefits, purposeful activities of university staff must involve actions that are focused on (1) the operating model, including required core processes, enabling systems and organisational function; (2) people and teams, including the allocation of the right combination of staff to different core processes; and (3) critical proficiencies. This latter aspect is integral to implementation.

People and teams: An effective implementation model must enable a process that grants universities the leeway and quick-fire flexibility to assemble teams in the face of opportunity, adversity and uncertainty. Teams of very different people must be brought together to deliver innovation, new programs and ground-breaking research projects, drawing on the organising functions of a university to get the job done. But given the seemingly endless complexity of the organisation that is a university, how is this achievable?

Here again, an understanding of both the factors that remain relatively constant and the variables that introduce elements of complexity is a sound starting place to determine the teams to bring together.

As presented earlier (Chapter 5, Critical Proficiencies), the proficiencies associated with deriving impact do not change, regardless of the internal and external environments. This is because socio-economic benefits materialise from universities in a fundamentally common way across all contexts (Chapter 2, Spheres of Impact). And, as explained earlier (Chapter 7, Operating Model), given that core processes are aligned with critical proficiencies, they, too, must remain relatively constant.

Operating contexts, on the other hand, are variable and dictate different leadership foci and decision-making frameworks, depending on how static or dynamic the environment is. In turn, a leader's focus regarding the management of people, deployment of resources, and ways to make critical decisions must change according to the operating context.

This influence of flux also extends to individual staff members and the composition of the teams set up to derive impact. The challenge here is to work out how best to harness the collective talents of staff members to drive great socio-economic benefits, and key to this is the distinction we now draw between the positions and the roles of university staff.

A _position_ is characterised as the function, responsibility and authority level of university staff within an existing organisational structure. Academic staff, for example, may hold positions that are senior, mid-career or early career across an array of academic units, such as faculties, schools or research institutes. General staff may hold positions that are senior, middle management or junior within the many organising functions of a university, such as teaching and learning support, research support, legal services, finance, marketing and communications, and facilities management. Executive staff may lead central units or key divisions, groups or faculties within universities. Differing aptitudes and attributes, and varying skills, knowledge and experience are associated with the function of each established position.

A *role*, on the other hand, is a task or job to which an individual may be assigned from time to time, as circumstances arise. A role can involve responsibilities within or across various elements of a university (e.g. a role on a steering committee assembled to address a university-wide issue). A role may also be temporary and allocated to a specific situation (e.g. the role of project leader on a team of staff assembled to undertake a one-off commercial research project). Each role requires individuals with different aptitudes and attributes, and varying degrees of expertise, knowledge and experience.

Universities must be prepared to create or activate a role according to the circumstances, or opportunities that arise. The attributes, skills and experience required for a given role must be identified and matched with the attributes, skills and experience associated with a certain position. In this way, a role typically requires a certain position as a prerequisite for assignment.

However, an individual holding a senior position may be assigned to a role where their expertise is optimal and required, but where they report to an individual who has the role of project leader, but whose position in the organisational structure is not necessarily classified as senior.

This example demonstrates an important flexibility that is created by the position/role distinction. University staff can be assigned to roles that vary with the changing shape of a university's opportunity spectrum. Such reassignments have no adverse implications for people who hold those positions, either in terms of remuneration or reward. This model also enables a university to handpick people in different positions when forming multi-disciplinary teams to deliver practical and innovative solutions, and ultimately socio-economic benefits.

Figure 36 (for illustration purposes only) shows various roles based on the key actions required to deliver socio-economic benefits (core processes) and the various elements within a university from which individuals in various positions can be drawn. These individuals can play key roles in some or several key actions. This mix-and-match approach framed around the core processes is integral to assembling the right teams for a given purpose.

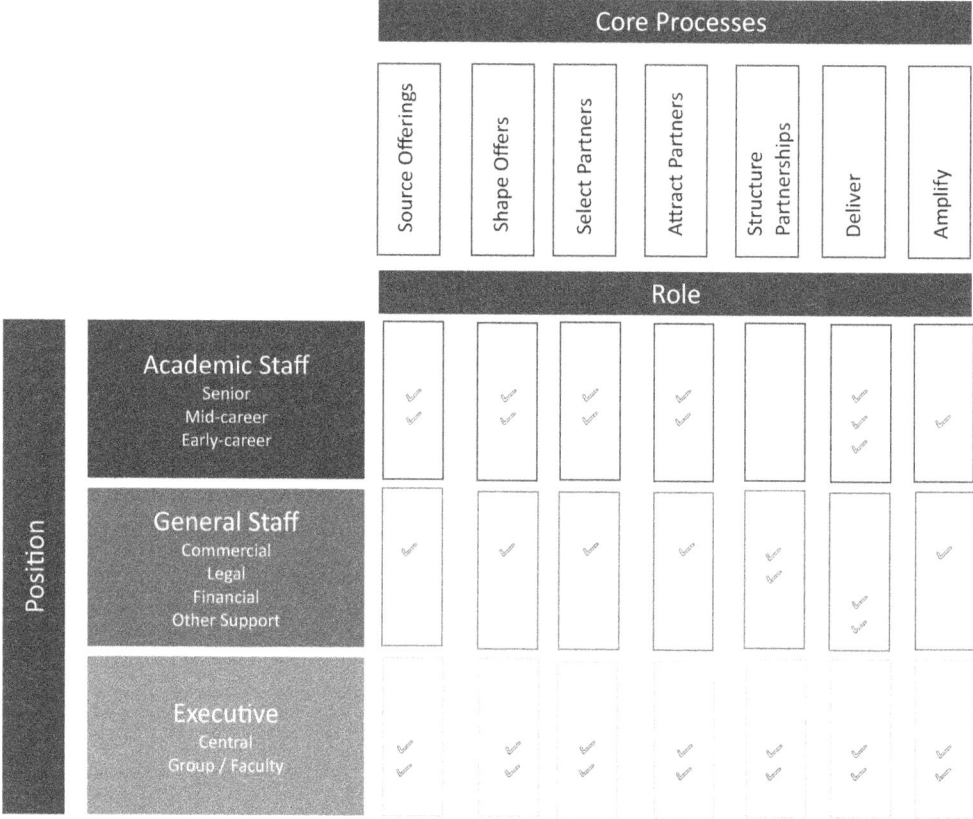

FIGURE 36: PROCESSES, POSITIONS AND ROLES

The process of selection and allocation must deliver a team fit for purpose, a group of individuals who can function collectively to meet the challenge at hand. The operating context in which this challenge is set must also guide the selection process as each operating context calls for a different set of skills, experience and attributes.

Defined operating contexts involve matters that universities do routinely. For example, many projects within a university are sourced, shaped and undertaken for an external partner by an academic staff member with the requisite expertise.

Engagement terms and conditions are typically negotiated with general staff who also have the requisite commercial experience. Performance is largely the responsibility of the academic staff member, as is managing the ongoing relationship with the external partner, and the development of further projects.

Complicated operating contexts involve multiple options for universities, calling for judicious selection. Here, engagements are typically sourced and undertaken by teams that include academic and general staff members (with the requisite expertise), often in partnership with several third parties. Partnership terms and conditions are negotiated with staff who have the requisite commercial experience. Performance is the responsibility of the academic teams, together with their partners. Commonly, relationship management involves leading academic and executive staff as a broad suite of university offerings are made available to partners, or in partnership.

Complex operating contexts involve universities navigating unpredictable and constantly changing circumstances. It requires a team of staff skilled at generating, testing and assessing opportunities, and rapidly marshalling resources in response to feedback. Opportunities are typically undertaken by teams of academic and general staff members (with commercial expertise), often in close consultation with executive and key stakeholders. Performance is the responsibility of the academic and commercial team, with oversight provided by executives. However, because of the dynamism of the environment, a team is responsible for continually navigating the environment with the aim of amplifying outcomes. The composition of teams is continually changing, as required by the capricious nature of a complex operating context. This represents a key difference between this context and the defined and complicated operating contexts in the selection and allocation process.

The ability to distinguish between position and role means a university can act efficiently in seamlessly assigning the right people to the right circumstance at exactly the right moment. It also offers another twofold benefit in the allocation of resources, and the attraction and retention of high-calibre staff. The distinction draws into focus the various contributions of staff—both academic and general—throughout the process of deriving socio-economic benefits, and it effectively calls for roles to be acknowledged and suitably rewarded, whether through remuneration and/or promotion to new positions.

The selection of individuals from certain positions for certain roles also reiterates the importance of informing, positioning and prioritising opportunities. In this way, the position/role distinction enables universities to prioritise the formation of teams around opportunities and partnerships that are likely to yield the greatest significant socio-economic impact. These opportunities can range from the many engagements associated with a relatively small proportion of cumulative revenues to a smaller number of large and significant engagements associated with most of the cumulative revenue (and impact). Irrespective of which end of this operational segment spectrum we consider, a mix of attributes, and the skills, knowledge and experience of staff, is paramount to success, and is enabled by a willingness and ability to adapt, guided by the distinction between position and role.

Accordingly, serving involves continually determining the key actions (core processes) required, the roles and associated attributes, skills, knowledge and experience required for those key actions, and the allocation of the right individuals from various positions to those roles. This is what enables extraordinary people to do extraordinary things.

The interplay between marshalling and serving

Implementation decisions involve detailed, creative and continual assessment, framed around a university's strategic decisions. Because strategic decisions change in response to a changing operating landscape, so, too, must implementation decisions change. The nature of the operating landscape associated with a university's strategic decisions also influences the operating context. This in turn determines the required leadership foci and decision-making frameworks that must be marshalled. Leadership foci and frameworks then determine the allocation of people and teams, and the utilisation of organisational functions that serve the needs of the university and its partners.

As illustrated in Figure 37, the activities of marshalling and serving work together to strategically allocate resources for the delivery of programs, products or services, and formation of partnerships that deliver great socio-economic benefits.

CAUSES   ACTIVITIES   EFFECTS

External Operating Context

Dimensions

- Defined: Certain or static, and
  therefore relatively predictable
- Complicated: Changeable or active,
  and therefore variable
- Complex: Uncertain or dynamic, and therefore
  relatively unpredictable
  ... as influenced by the external
  operating landscape including:
  - Societal factors
  - Industry factors
  ... which determine required leadership
  foci and decision-making frameworks.

Marshalling

Academic Impact

Tangible educational programs
and research outcomes
('offerings')

Collaborative Impact

Delivery of programs, products
or services to the community
('partnerships')

Internal Operating Context

People and Teams

- Required 'roles', shaped around core processes
- Required 'positions', based on skills, experience
  and attributes, and matched to roles

Engagement Model

- Objective, purpose, focus
- Internal and external channels

Operating Model

- Core processes
- Enabling systems
- Organisational functions

Serving

Societal Impact

Impact on the community
from utilising the
programs or products or
receiving the services
('socio-economic benefits')

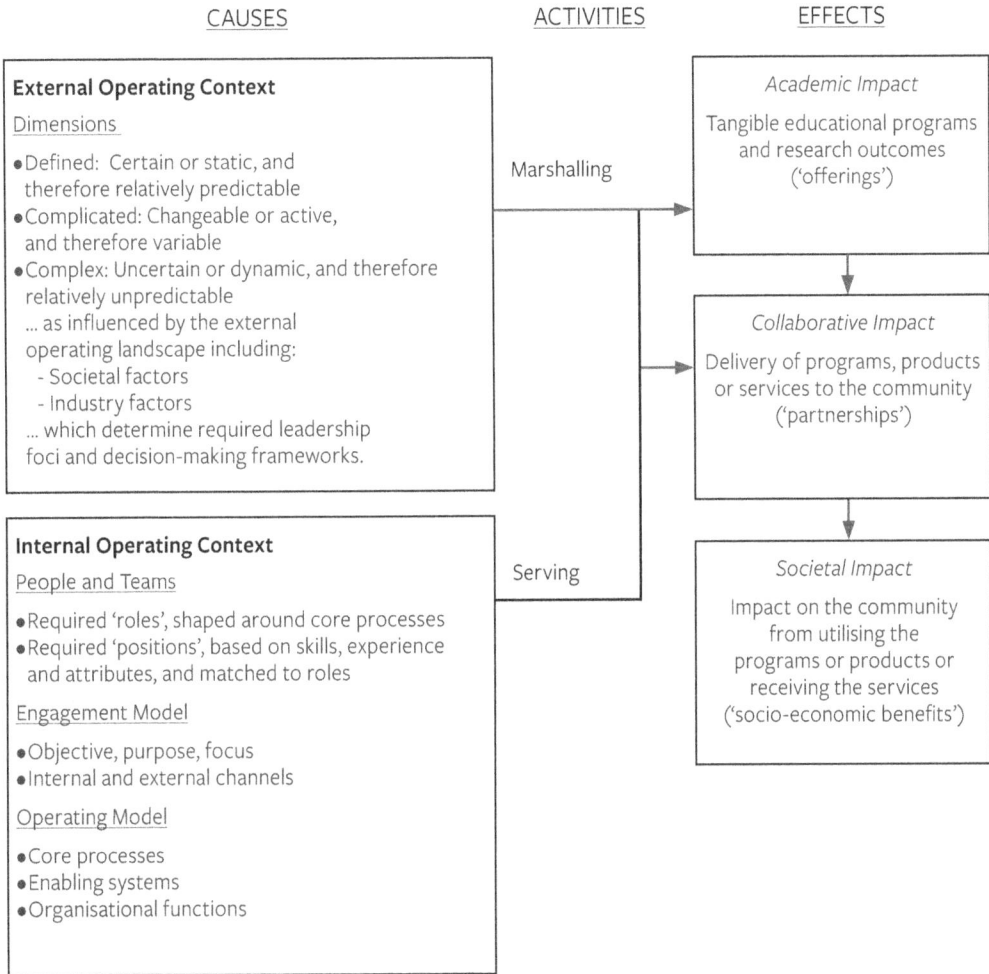

FIGURE 37: THE INTERPLAY BETWEEN MARSHALLING AND SERVING

The garnering and imparting of information to support associated decisions and activities are undertaken through purposeful engagement utilising various engagement channels. So, in a similar way to the activities of sensing and sourcing, the activities of marshalling and serving are inextricably linked.

Gelling strategic decisions and implementation decisions requires an activity in its own right: harmonising. This brings together the activities of sensing, sourcing, marshalling and serving. In a sense, harmonising is at the heart of any organisation and therefore integral to its success.

HARMONISING

At the very core of the implementation model detailed in this chapter are people, and the challenge of how to gel people together into a cohesive whole.

Harmonising, as stated earlier, reflects the abilities of people within an organisation to link insights and ideas, and to draw together assets and resources and direct them toward meeting the needs and wants of their stakeholders. It is the specific process by which context is created in order for an organisation's people to pull all activities together. And, as argued throughout, for universities focused on deriving impact, all purposeful activities should be creatively, constructively and consistently focused on the critical proficiencies (what we need to be good at): how to curate opportunities, shape enduring partnerships, and deliver great socio-economic benefits.

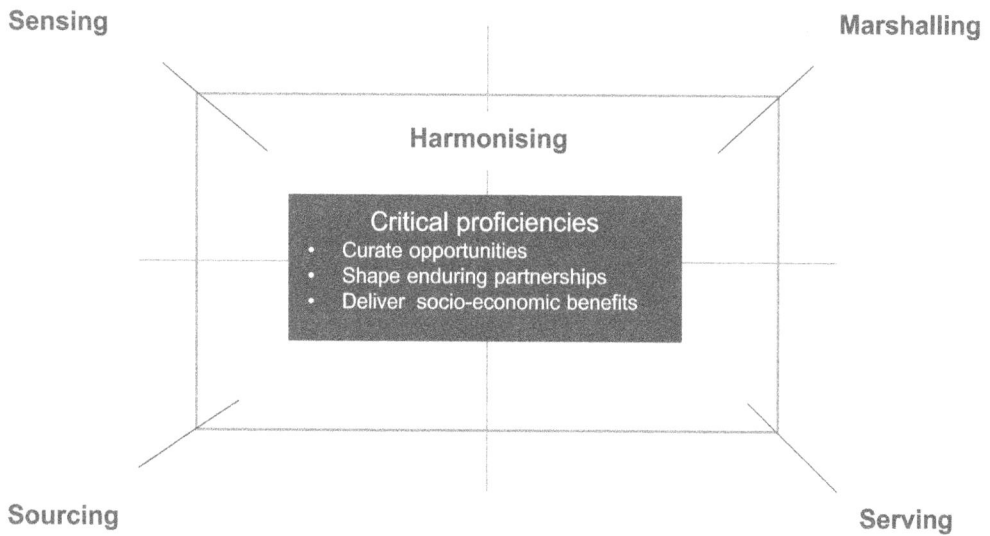

FIGURE 38: HARMONISING (REALM 5)

Importantly, universities (indeed, all organisations) are open systems, where information must travel in and out and within to aid decision-making, instruct activities, and attract and convert opportunities to meaningful outcomes. Therefore, a key component of harmonisation involves strategic conversations, those two-way exchanges (speaking and listening) between key stakeholders (internal and external) that are framed around the components of the implementation model described in this chapter.

Within the context of an implementation model, harmonising clearly benefits from the embedding of meaningful values that help people make the right choices, and that guide behaviours. This embedment is a process of involving people in the choices that must be made (strategic decisions) and the actions required to convert those choices to outcomes (implementation decisions). People must be empowered to do extraordinary things. For optimal results where the goal is societal benefit, all efforts must be aligned and the values that guide behaviours must play a binding role.

Strategic conversations

Deriving impact from universities involves conversations between many stakeholders. Conversation is a two-way exchange. To be strategic, conversations must focus on the key components assembled in each realm of the implementation model, including the factors that anchor all decision-making for universities, and the associated approaches to utilise when making those decisions.

Harmonising involves obtaining and imparting the necessary information at the right times and with the right people so that strategic decisions and implementation decisions are effective. Harmonising fuses purposeful engagement and purposeful activities through strategic conversations. Only through the continual hum of strategic conversations—the valuable, ongoing interactions induced by an involved, coordinated and encompassing university climate, where the modes of communication are fluid and their content rich and real—can harmonisation occur.

Bringing activities together, therefore, requires the right conversations and actions at the right time involving the right people. In the context of an implementation model, these are *strategic* conversations, conduits to determining what needs to be discussed; who must be informed, addressed or persuaded (internal or external); what each audience needs to know; how each audience is best reached; and what is required from each audience. From these strategic conversations emerge tangible activities with goals (the results that are required); priorities (the high-impact issues that must be addressed); requirements (the specific resources required for each priority); actions (the key actions that must be taken for each priority); and responsibilities (who takes the actions and by when).

Strategic conversations recognise the uncertainty of operating environments, and how instantly redundant one-way directives driven by thick, turgid strategic documents can be. In a dynamic environment, such documents are predicated on a suite of assumptions that may be rendered invalid as soon as they are proofread. They inevitably lose relevance in the maelstrom of day-to-day challenges faced when running an organisation. In our rapidly changing environments, continual informed actions around common purposes are required to drive results. Accepting this premise means staff and university partners need to be involved in important issues, and have continuing roles and input in strategic and implementation decision-making. At the same time, university leaders need to spend time 'in the trenches'; in the company of clever, well-informed people, constantly engaged in the purposeful activities that forge tangible outcomes.

Harmonisation requires the involvement of staff and is fused by strategic conversations. Involvement must of course be aligned with organisational direction. Values that help people make the right choices and that guide behaviours enhance this alignment.

Values and behaviours

Values help an organisation define who they are, who they aspire to be, and how they work together. Where values are true, they are idiosyncratic and peculiar to an organisation. They must represent people's choices which inherently relate to organisational direction. Values are the guiding principles that shape actions that inform and fulfil organisational direction. They can be utilised by universities to frame the organisational policies that lay out the obligations of their people, and to set expectations for the behaviours of all organisational staff. When they are effective, values guide behaviours and help people make the right choices. Accordingly, values and behaviours are an integral component of harmonisation.

Values should not be confused with virtues or beliefs. It is relatively easy to build a consensus around generic virtues such as excellence, respect, integrity and communication.[3] These can be applied to any organisation in the world, but it is not unusual for them to be meaningless and amount to little more than noisy lip service. We must ask how values become more than lip service.

Values become meaningful, embedded and aligned with deriving impact from universities when they are developed through the implementation-model framework, an effective tool in showing: (a) how and why values guide choice of behaviour and (b) alignments between values and activities. Importantly, values and behaviours must be framed around what people need to *do*, not what people need to *think*. They must reflect the nature of the choices that have to be made (strategic decisions) and the actions required to convert those choices into outcomes (implementation decisions). They must consider the factors that anchor all decision-making and the associated approaches that help frame the required information and actions. In that way, despite the continually changing operating landscapes and contexts that universities face, their people are more likely to focus on the important things that need to be achieved, and in so doing act in ways that are more likely to derive impact.

Focusing on the four distinct realms within the implementation-model framework enables a thematic function to be attached to each realm. For example, to realm one, which combines intent, opportunity spectrum and critical proficiencies, may be ascribed the thematic function *improve our world*. Similarly, to realm two may be ascribed *shape the way* (combining operating model, understanding the knowledge-capital value chain and critical proficiencies). To realm three may be ascribed *make a difference* (combining intent, leadership foci, and decision-making frameworks and critical proficiencies). And to realm four could be ascribed *here to help* (combining operating model, people and teams, and critical proficiencies).

Strategy   Implementation

Realm 1: Sensing   **Intent**   Realm 3: Marshalling
                          • North stars
                          • Spheres of impact

Major influences (operating landscape)

External factors

Opportunity Spectrum   Leadership foci and Decision-making framework

External factors

5. Harmonising

Improve our world   *Make a difference*

Critical proficiencies
• Curate opportunities
• Shape enduring partnerships
• Deliver socio-economic benefits

Shape the way   *Here to help*

Internal factors

Knowledge-capital Value Chain   People and teams

Internal factors

Major influences (operating context)

Operating Model
• Core processes
• Enabling systems
• Organisational functions

Realm 2: Sourcing   Realm 4: Serving

Purposeful Engagement

Strategy   Implementation

Nature of Decisions

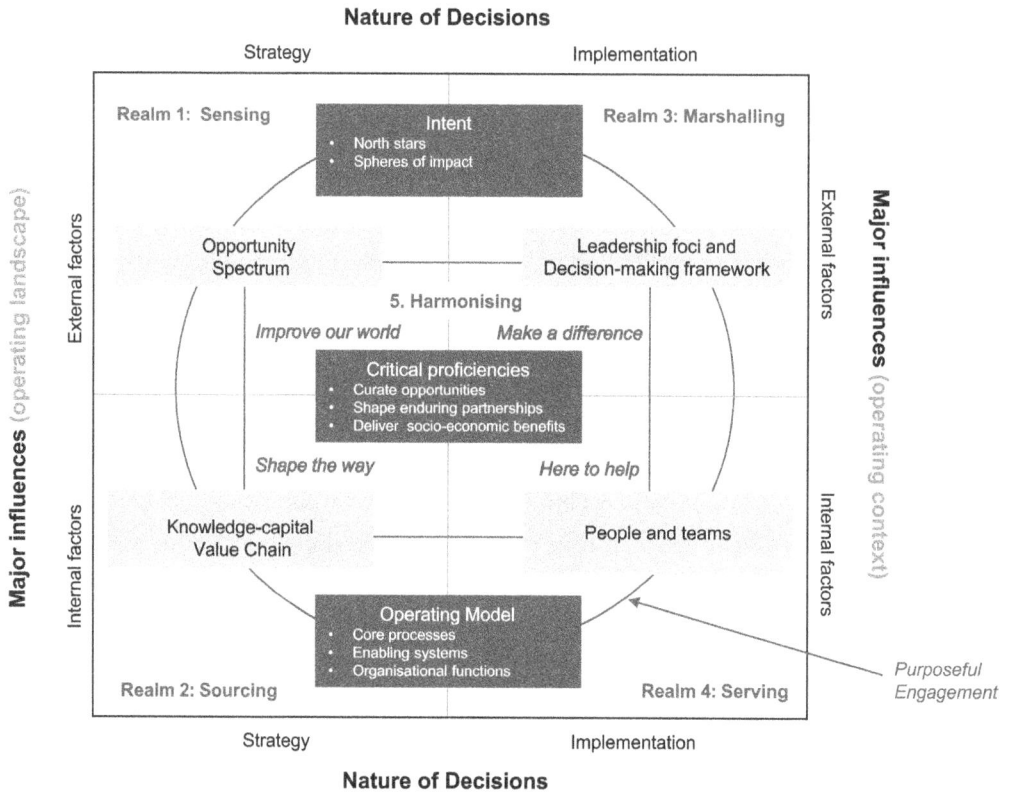

FIGURE 39: VALUES AND BEHAVIOURS SUPPORTING DECISION-MAKING

By focusing on the key concepts in each realm, values can be aligned with suitable university activities. For example, realm one focuses on why universities exist, and it may ultimately be utilised by universities seeking to derive impact to align values and behaviours with a focus on those in need, finding solutions to related issues, and driving enduring outcomes.

Realm two focuses on why universities need to work with the best partners, and this realm may ultimately be utilised to align values and behaviours with identifying and selecting the best resources and partners, and driving enduring partnerships that can deliver great socio-economic benefits.

Realm three focuses on the way universities work with key stakeholders to achieve the derivation of great socio-economic benefits, and may ultimately be utilised to align values and behaviours with the need to be proactive, innovative, collaborative and judicious.

Realm four focuses on how universities must work together with partners, and can be ultimately utilised to align values and behaviours with the importance of valuing relationships, working together with common purpose, and being trusted partners.

The process of crafting meaningful values for each realm requires an understanding of the specifics of the dominion, key factors and objectives at play within that dominion, and how purposeful engagement is applied to derive the values that inform decision-making. This application of purposeful engagement is an important part of this process and one that harmonises purposeful activities within a university.

ESTABLISHING AN IMPLEMENTATION MODEL

The establishment of an implementation model requires a level of coherence and coordination underwritten by human drive. We have seen how this nurtures an ability to sense change and adapt, how it guides the allocation of expertise to the tasks thrown up by turbulent times, and how it forges key values that guide the behaviour and actions of staff.

When decisions around strategy and implementation are at hand, it is ultimately the array of talented, knowledgeable, innovative and experienced people within universities that determines how universities choose what to do (strategy), and how they get that job done (implementation). Motivation of staff is unlocked from within; they must want to act and perform. Therefore, university leaders must create a climate in which people motivate themselves to help the university achieve its intent. Organisations work when they maximise the chance that each person, working with others, will grow and contribute to the common good.

In conclusion, continually considering the following questions helps universities build a climate to support the derivation of impact:

Question 1: What key system-based activities are called for?
Question 2: What purposeful engagement is required?
Question 3: What purposeful activities are needed?
Question 4: What leadership and decision-making framework is appropriate?
Question 5: Which people and teams are essential?
Question 6: What strategic conversations are vital?
Question 7: What values will support coherent and aligned decision-making?

This completes the development of an implementation model to assist a university to derive impact. In a time of environmental complexity, rapid change, heightening competition and hyper-connectedness, competitive advantage depends more and more on building an organisation that can act. Armed with an understanding of the critical components that set organisational direction and guide organisational character, we now progress to the final chapter, which lays out an ecosystem approach.

Chapter 8 Endnotes

1. Complex environments are also experienced with so-called 'black swan' events (e.g. pandemic), which less frequently occur, but which precipitate very fluid environments.
2. Success in complex operating contexts is about learning fast, not failing fast. The latter expression, in my view, is unhelpful as it can connote an opportunistic rather than a considered approach to experimentation and testing the market.
3. For those interested, these 'virtues' were the corporate values of Enron (2000 annual report). As events have shown, they were not meaningful or deeply ingrained principles that shaped actions and helped people make the right choices.

CHAPTER 9

DEVELOPING AN ECOSYSTEM

'The whole is more than the sum of its parts.'

—Aristotle

KEY THEMES

- Understanding how ecosystems function as an all-encompassing matrix

- Understanding that fundamentals of the framework are constant, irrespective of stage of development

- Applying functionality of the framework across the organisation, regardless of strategic or tactical orientation

- Using uniformity to generate increasingly sophisticated and targeted approaches over time

Across the preceding chapters, we have constructed a novel framework for the times that is aimed at calibrating university operations. It takes into consideration the resources at a university's disposal, and ways of keeping a handle on an institution's bearings in dynamic and competitive environments. The thinking has always been guided by the goal of societal benefit, and how universities in the 21st century go about deriving the most effective impact.

In this final chapter, how ecosystems can serve the grand plan is described. In adopting an ecosystem approach, each individual university embraces the reality of its own operating landscape and operating contexts. Using the framework, each university can create a perfect harmony of concepts that interplay relentlessly in the production and reproduction of organisational direction and organisational character. In developing its own ecosystem, each university stares down the barrel of unprecedented, apparently insurmountable complexity, and navigates a way forward to deliver even better outcomes that benefit our societies.

SETTING UP AN ECOSYSTEM APPROACH

By utilising the deriving-impact framework, a university can peer through the white noise of uncertain and dynamic environments, and consistently pare back to basics to establish intent through setting direction and generating purpose. It also enables the university to maintain focus by consistently combining an understanding of the knowledge-capital value chain with discernment of an opportunity spectrum. Intent and focus (deciding what to do) are two concepts at the framework's conceptual core. They have a predominantly strategic orientation and put universities into position to take a proactive approach to the identification of what we call '*priority opportunities*'.

Three other concepts—curate, shape, deliver—relate to what we need to be adept at doing: those activities in which a university must have expertise (critical proficiencies). These have a predominantly tactical orientation. A university that curates is one that works out ways to enlist and activate expertise, utilise research capabilities, and advance innovations. In the act of curating, a university converts *priority* opportunities to *tangible* opportunities. A university that shapes is one that generates mutually beneficial engagements with an external partner to address a societal need. In the act of shaping, a university progresses tangible opportunities into active partnerships capable of deriving impact.

In a university, this process of identifying priority opportunities, curating tangible opportunities, shaping active partnerships, and delivering optimum socio-economic impact works in sync with a combination of the engagement, operating and implementation models. It is an all-encompassing matrix of interrelated processes whereby a university's activities, methods, policies, decision-makers and teams coexist and go about their business with a consistency that prevails in an uncertain external environment. This community of interacting university professionals and processes is the lifeblood of an ecosystem approach.

Importantly, it is a relentless process. The successful delivery of a product that benefits society is a goal but never the *end* goal, as each process regenerates, circling back to intent and focus, again deciding what to do, but now curating a new suite of opportunities to pursue with the benefit of advanced partnerships and repeated relationships. Over time, complexity, richness and efficiency are incrementally incorporated into the process, drawing on new and different parts of university expertise, and generating the possibility of multiple, customised and targeted societal benefits. In this way, the process not only provides the lifeblood but also builds the ecosystem.

Further development and understanding of an ecosystem approach are made possible through deeper analysis of (1) priority opportunities, (2) tangible opportunities, (3) active partnerships, and (4) deriving impact and related processes.

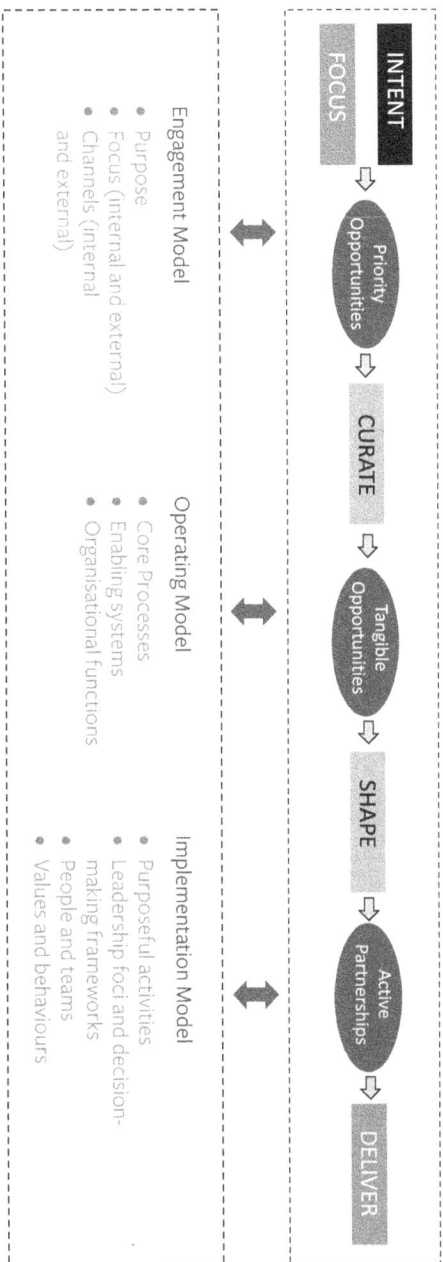

FIGURE 40: SETTING UP AN ECOSYSTEM APPROACH

INTENT
FOCUS

⇩

Priority Opportunities

⇩

CURATE

⇩

Tangible Opportunities

⇩

SHAPE

⇩

Active Partnerships

⇩

DELIVER

Engagement Model
- Purpose
- Focus (internal and external)
- Channels (internal and external)

Operating Model
- Core Processes
- Enabling systems
- Organisational functions

Implementation Model
- Purposeful activities
- Leadership foci and decision-making frameworks
- People and teams
- Values and behaviours

PRIORITY OPPORTUNITIES

Discerning a set of priority opportunities requires four key constituents, the first being direction. Here, a cursory examination of major trends and demographic shifts is informative with regard to the changing nature of (1) workforces, (2) the sharp rise in entrepreneurship, and (3) the catalogue of enduring and emerging societal needs towards which a university may aspire and direct activities. These are the north stars, which are constant regardless of the dynamism of the environments in which any university operates. Universities seeking to derive impact should frame opportunities and establish direction around these.

The second constituent involves the establishment of purpose. Here, universities galvanise action by focusing on (1) societal needs, (2) organising solutions that address societal needs, and (3) establishing partnerships capable of delivering significant societal benefits.

Understanding the knowledge-capital value chain, the third constituent brings to light the attributes of priority opportunities and the various approaches required to advance them. Therefore, a university must have comprehensive knowledge of the nature of underlying assets, the different markets these assets address, the various paths-to-markets, and the possible delivery mechanisms. This knowledge guides the use of a university's full suite of assets (e.g. knowledge, research capabilities, innovations) and how these may converge in collaboration and partnership with external organisations to deliver the greatest possible impact.

Finally, universities must discern their opportunity spectrums to ensure that they pursue opportunities consistent with their directions, purposes and core strategies; they are competitively positioned and prioritised; and they are likely to derive the most impact from available resource envelopes.

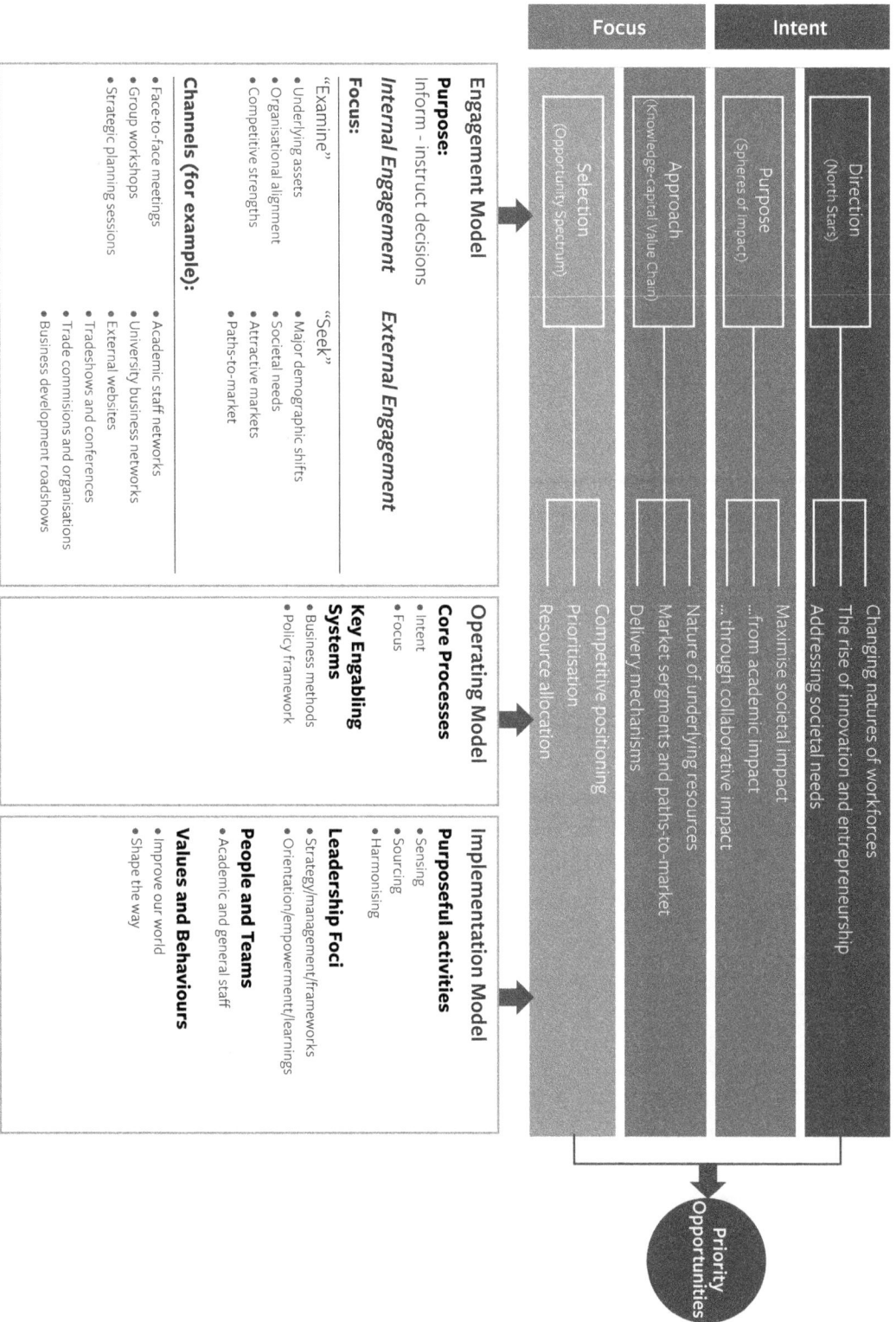

Focus | **Intent**

Selection
(Opportunity Spectrum)

Approach
(Knowledge-capital Value Chain)

Purpose
(Spheres of impact)

Direction
(North Stars)

Engagement Model

Purpose:
Inform - instruct decisions

Internal Engagement

Focus:
"Examine"
- Underlying assets
- Organisational alignment
- Competitive strengths

External Engagement
"Seek"
- Major demographic shifts
- Societal needs
- Attractive markets
- Paths-to-market

Channels (for example):
- Face-to-face meetings
- Group workshops
- Strategic planning sessions
- Academic staff networks
- University business networks
- External websites
- Tradeshows and conferences
- Trade commisions and organisations
- Business development roadshows

Operating Model

Core Processes
- Intent
- Focus

Key Engabling Systems
- Business methods
- Policy framework

Competitive positioning
Prioritisation
Resource allocation

Delivery mechanisms
Market sergments and paths-to-market
Nature of underlying resources

Maximise societal impact
...from academic impact
...through collaborative impact

Changing natures of workforces
The rise of innovation and entrepreneurship
Addressing societal needs

Implementation Model

Purposeful activities
- Sensing
- Sourcing
- Harmonising

Leadership Foci
- Strategy/management/frameworks
- Orientation/empowerment/learnings

People and Teams
- Academic and general staff

Values and Behaviours
- Improve our world
- Shape the way

Priority Opportunities

The careful, informed judgement of priority opportunities takes place within the all-encompassing matrix of interrelated processes, presented in Figure 41, and it is here that the engagement model takes its place among the pulleys and levers in the engine room of the matrix. In this context, the key purpose of engagement is to inform decisions. The focus of internal engagement is to examine factors such as underlying assets, organisational alignment, delivery mechanisms and competitive strengths. The focus of external engagement is to seek elements like major demographic shifts, societal needs, and attractive markets and paths to those markets, including potential partners. Various engagement channels that facilitate this purpose are required. Supporting this are various enabling systems (e.g. activities, programs, methods), particularly business methods and policy framework.

Typically, the operating context is changeable, variable and active, and leadership focuses on strategy, management and frameworks that help garner information, assess it, analyse options and select courses of action. A strategic orientation means executive and senior staff are often involved, with values focused on improving our world and shaping the way. Associated purposeful activities are aligned predominantly with sensing what is occurring, sourcing key resources, and harmonising activities across differing contexts.

TANGIBLE OPPORTUNITIES

In converting priority opportunities to tangible opportunities, universities near a point where they have assembled the relevant resources and worked through the process of partner identification. This involves different aspects of an engagement model, operating model and implementation model, as presented in Figure 42.

Priority Opportunities

Curate

Tangible Opportunities

Engagement Model

Purpose:
Enlist – source and design offerings to facilitate uptake and utilisation

Internal Engagement   External Engagement

Focus:

"Activate"
- Orient and deploy resources to provide solutions

"Understand"
- Identify and articulate the problem to solve

Channels (for example):
- Face-to-face meetings
- Internal events
- Digital/online support
- Seminars
- Concept development
- Academic staff networks
- University business networks
- External websites
- Tradeshows and conferences
- Trade commissions and organisations
- Business development roadshows
- Peer exchange
- Third-party brokers

Operating Model

Core Processes
- Source offerings
- Shape offers
- Select partners

Key Enabling Systems
- Business methods
- Policy framework
- Training programs
- Investment programs
- Outreach programs

Implementation Model

Purposeful activities
- Marshalling
- Sourcing
- Harmonising

Leadership Foci
- Strategy/management/frameworks
- Orientation/empowerment/learnings

People and Teams
- Academic and general staff

Values and Behaviours
- Shape the way
- Make a difference

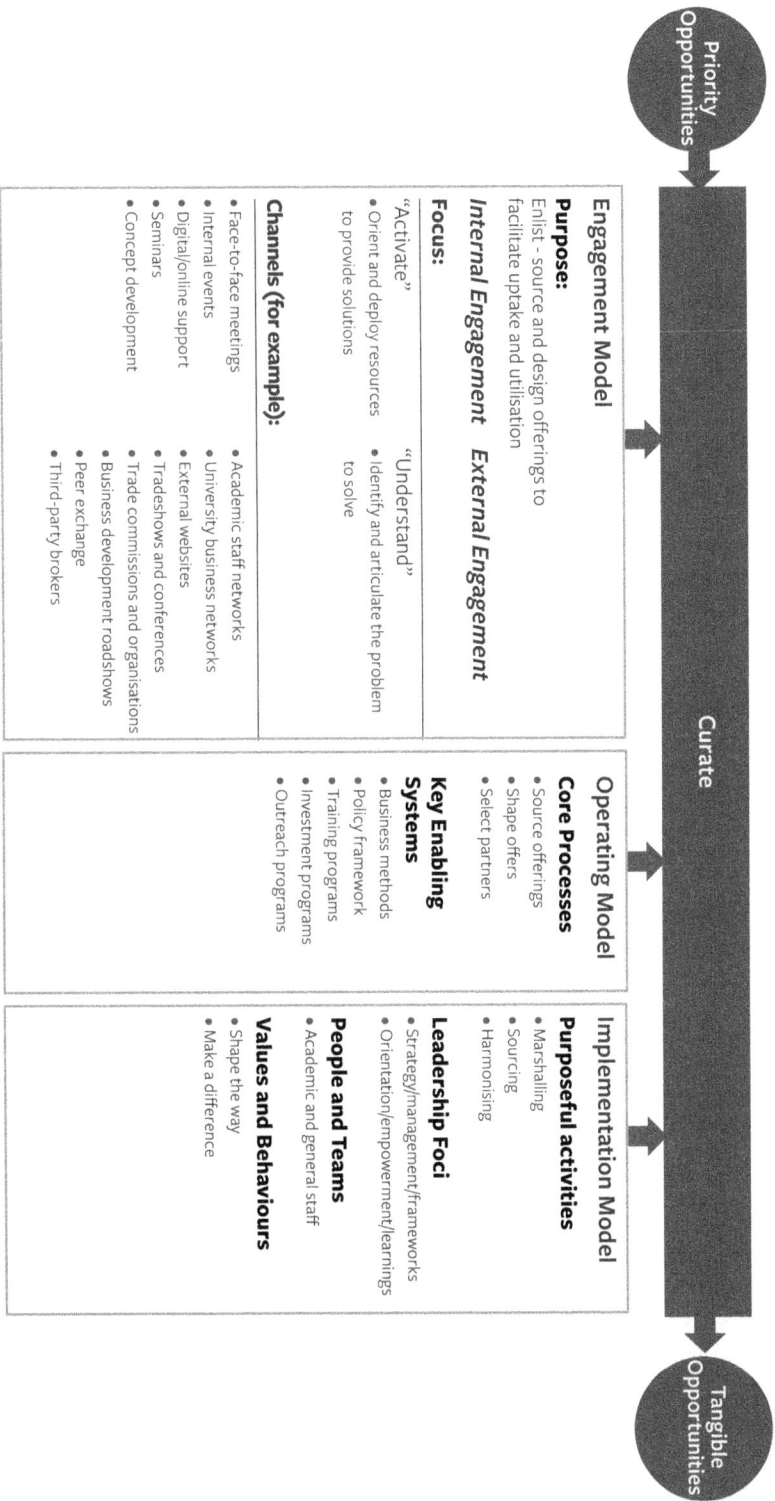

FIGURE 42: MOVING FROM PRIORITY OPPORTUNITIES TO TANGIBLE OPPORTUNITIES

The key purpose of engagement shifts to enlisting, with external engagement focused on understanding the nature of problems; and internal engagement focused on activating solutions, again utilising various channels for engagement. Core processes—the key actions required—are centred on sourcing offerings, shaping offers, and identifying the best partners with the help of enabling programs that include business methods; policy framework; and training, investment and outreach programs.

The operating context can span from changeable, variable and active on one side, to uncertain, unpredictable and dynamic on the other side. The focus of leadership therefore extends across strategy, management and frameworks, and continues to orientation, empowerment and learnings. This supports the garnering of information and specifying of actions required to advance toward potential partnerships. Here a range of academic and general staff is often involved, with values driven by shaping the way and making a difference. Here, purposeful activities predominantly involve sourcing key resources, marshalling multiple stakeholders, and harmonising across various divergent stakeholders.

ACTIVE PARTNERSHIPS

Progressing tangible opportunities to active partnerships again sees different aspects of engagement, operating and implementation models at play, as presented in Figure 43. The key purpose of engagement shifts to structuring partnerships, with internal engagement focused on crafting value propositions, including the right partners; and external engagement focused on understanding the problem to solve, and the job of attracting the best partners.

Tangible Opportunities

Shape

Active Partnerships

Engagement Model

Purpose:
Structure - shape mutually beneficial and sustainable partnerships

Internal Engagement   External Engagement

Focus:

"Craft"
• Develop value propositions

"Attract"
• Explore mutually beneficial arrangements

Channels (for example):
• Face-to-face meetings
• Internal workshops
• Academic staff networks
• University business networks
• External websites
• Tradeshows and conferences
• Trade commissions and organisations
• Business development roadshows
• Peer exchange
• Third-party brokers

Operating Model

Core Processes
• Select partners
• Attract partners
• Structure and enter partnerships

Key Enabling Systems
• Business methods
• Policy framework
• Training programs
• Investment programs
• Outreach programs

Implementation Model

Purposeful activities
• Marshalling
• Sourcing
• Harmonising

Leadership Foci
• Strategy/management/frameworks
• Orientation/empowerment/learnings

People and Teams
• Academic and general staff

Values and Behaviours
• Shape the way
• Make a difference

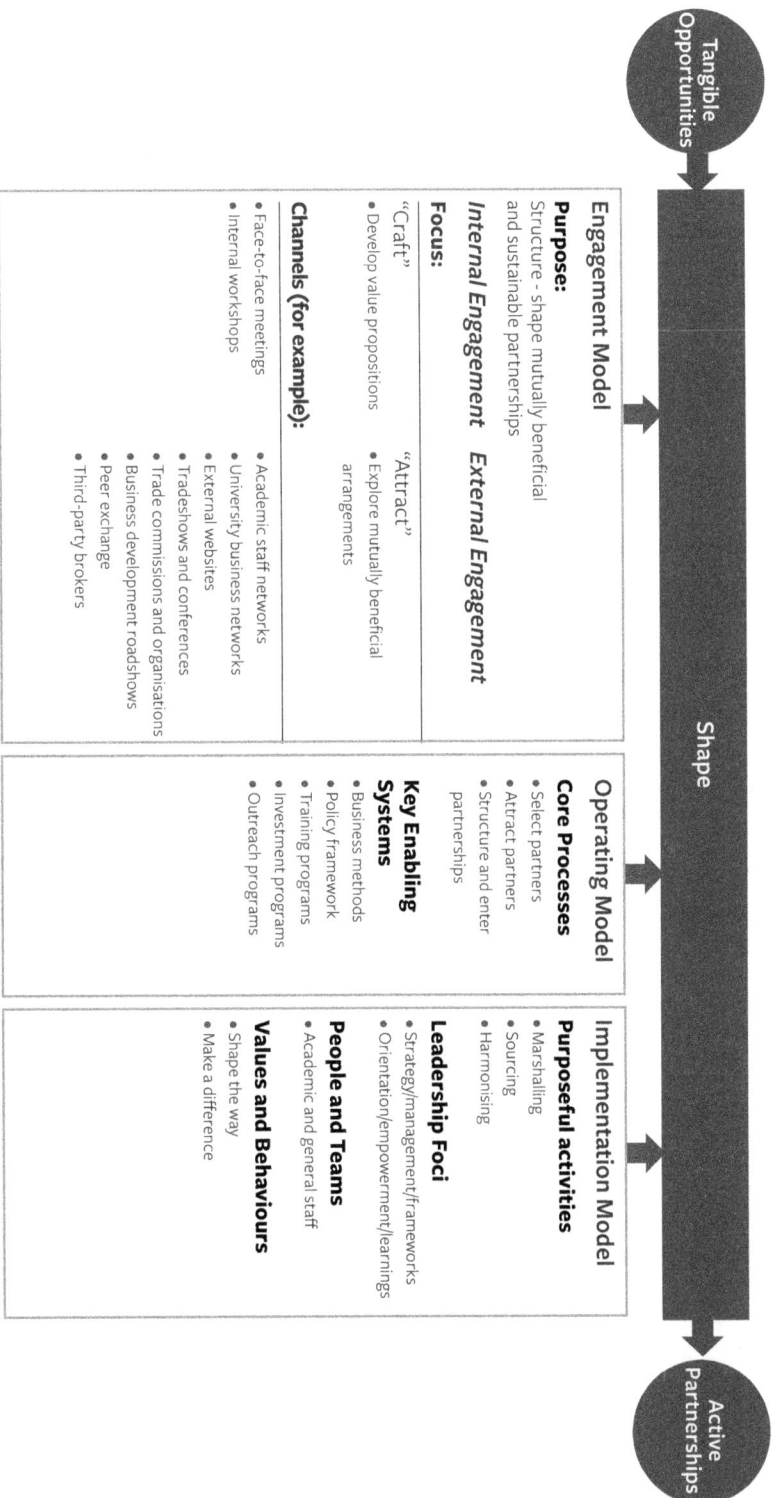

FIGURE 43: MOVING FROM TANGIBLE OPPORTUNITIES TO ACTIVE PARTNERSHIPS

Core processes are all about partner selection, attracting partners and structuring partnerships. Again, in support are a suite of enabling programs including business methods; policy framework; and training, investment and outreach programs. Also again, the operating context is typically changeable, variable and active, with leadership focused on strategy, management and frameworks. A range of academic and general staff is involved, with values focused on making a difference and shaping the way. Purposeful activities predominantly involve sourcing key resources, marshalling multiple stakeholders, and harmonising interests.

DERIVING IMPACT

To derive impact by converting active partnerships into great socio-economic benefits involves different aspects of the engagement, operating and implementation models, as presented in Figure 44. The key purpose of engagement now shifts to performing in partnership, with internal engagement focused on managing a university's contributions, and external engagement focused on leveraging partners to amplify outcomes. Core processes focus on the agreed partnership, delivery of outcomes, and amplification of those outcomes to drive great socio-economic outcomes. In support is a suite of enabling programs including business methods; policy framework; and training, investment and outreach programs.

Here, the operating context typically ranges from certain, predictable and static to changeable, variable and active. Leadership foci therefore reach from objectives and goals, skills and processes, to strategy, management and frameworks. Here a mixture of academic and general staff works together with staff from the partner organisations involved. Values are focused on how to improve our world, make a difference, and being here to help. Purposeful activities predominantly involve marshalling multiple stakeholders, serving partners and the community, and harmonising interests.

Engagement Model

Purpose:
Perform - ensure the most in need get benefits through the provisions of solutions

Internal Engagement   External Engagement

Focus:

"Manage"
- Guide successful delivery of solutions

"Leverage"
- Work with partners to amplify outcomes

Channels (for example):

- Face-to-face meetings
- Peer exchange
- Project management and reporting

- Commercial partners attraction program
- Strategic partnerships
- Peer exchange programs
- Third-party broker
- Piggy-backing (joint bids)

Operating Model

Core Processes
- Structure partnerships
- Deliver outcomes
- Amplify

Key Enabling Systems
- Business methods
- Policy framework
- Training programs
- Investment programs
- Outreach programs

Implementation Model

Purposeful activities
- Marshalling
- Sourcing
- Harmonising

Leadership Foci
- Strategy/management/frameworks
- Orientation/empowerment/learnings

People and Teams
- Academic and general staff

Values and Behaviours
- Make a difference
- Here to help

Active Opportunities

Deliver

Socio-economic benefits

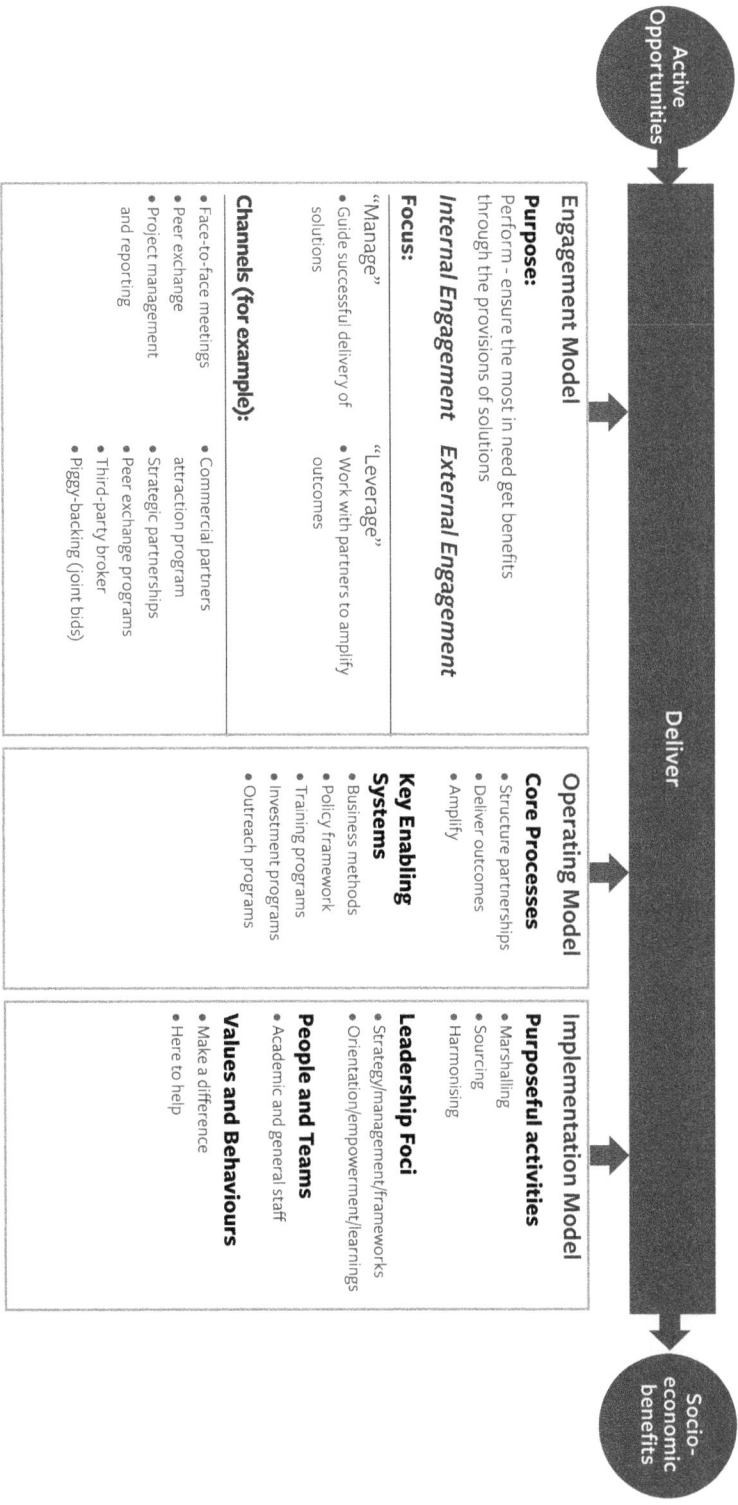

FIGURE 44: MOVING FROM ACTIVE PARTNERSHIPS TO SOCIO-ECONOMIC BENEFITS

TOWARDS AN ECOSYSTEM APPROACH

In the above discussion and development of an ecosystem approach, the core concepts of *intent, focus, curate, shape* and *deliver* are effectively brought to life at one and the same time. These concepts go to work in an ecosystem where priority opportunities are converted into tangible opportunities, and where tangible opportunities progress to active partnerships that are advanced and sustained to derive impact that benefits society. In practical terms, enabling programs such as highly organised internal-engagement programs are developed to facilitate outcomes. These may include support services like practitioner-led education and training, and investment programs like proof-of-concept funds, seed-capital funds, and in some instances venture-capital funds (either directly or through alliances). In addition, outreach programs can be nuanced to include refined external-engagement programs. These may include strategic partnerships with industry, government and community, and significant external investment.

Crucially, the fundamentals of the framework remain the same at all times, irrespective of stage of development. The functionality of the framework to derive impact is applied consistently across the depth and span of the organisation, regardless of strategic or tactical orientation (as depicted in Figure 45). Through this uniformity in approach and its relentless application universities generate increasingly sophisticated and targeted approaches over the course of time.

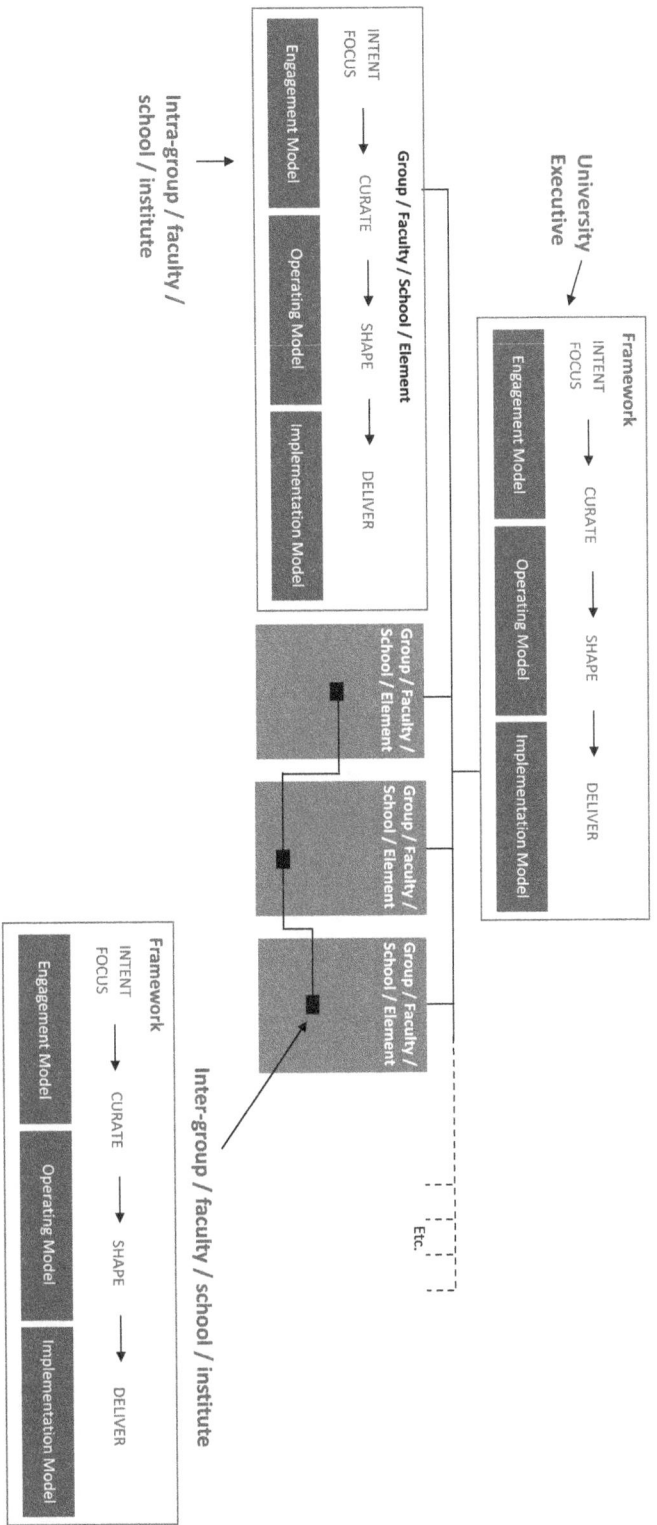

FIGURE 45: TOWARDS AN ECOSYSTEM APPROACH

CONCLUSION

Universities are bubbling with people full of fresh ideas and innovative solutions. These are leaders, academics, researchers and professionals who see our new century as a time of extraordinary opportunity. They embrace it with all its complexity and uncertainty. They are highly valued by the broader community outside the university domain. Business leaders, entrepreneurs, governments and students of the world seek out their knowledge and expertise, often with the intention of bettering society.

While the delivery of such socio-economic benefits has forever been a part of the university manifesto, successful universities of our new century recognise that delivering benefits now hinges on business-model design and implementation capability: the need for action. These are the universities that put resources to their best use, get results quickly, learn by doing, and make strategy and change simultaneous activities. For these universities, strategy is change and change is strategy. These are the universities that actively shift resources to address market needs, evolving with new trends, demographic shifts, and changing funding models and economic conditions. And while they adapt and respond to the world and its uncertain ways, they maintain a consistency in their business practices.

The framework to derive impact presented here provides a blueprint for such consistent, unequivocal application of process. It checks the headstrong instinct to pursue one type of engagement (e.g. start-ups) without prior understanding of a university's knowledge-capital value chain. It averts a loss of direction when resources are rationed. It prompts consistent internal engagement aimed at preliminary development of products and services that may be future solutions. In this way, the potential societal benefit is nurtured, with enabling programs enlisting, activating and ultimately advancing products and services to a stage where they are capable of delivery to the community.

Outreach programs advance the process by identifying and engaging with industry partners, without whom expansive delivery does not happen. This involves strategic partnerships, the connection point where collaboration on a service or product turns idea into prototype into product or service utilised by the community. It also involves external investment, where the funding to translate products and services to wide-scale delivery is achieved.

The framework paves the way for meaningful and sustainable connections with business leaders, entrepreneurs, governments, partners, and future leaders in the guise of students. It fosters a dynamic between the university sector and the commercial business world, and produces and delivers the best ideas to the world in a way that makes a difference.

We conclude with a renewed hope, optimistic that *The University Imperative* has delivered on its promise to provide a useful framework for universities to calibrate their operations, and future-proof the tremendous social dividend they have historically contributed to our world, so they continue well into the future.

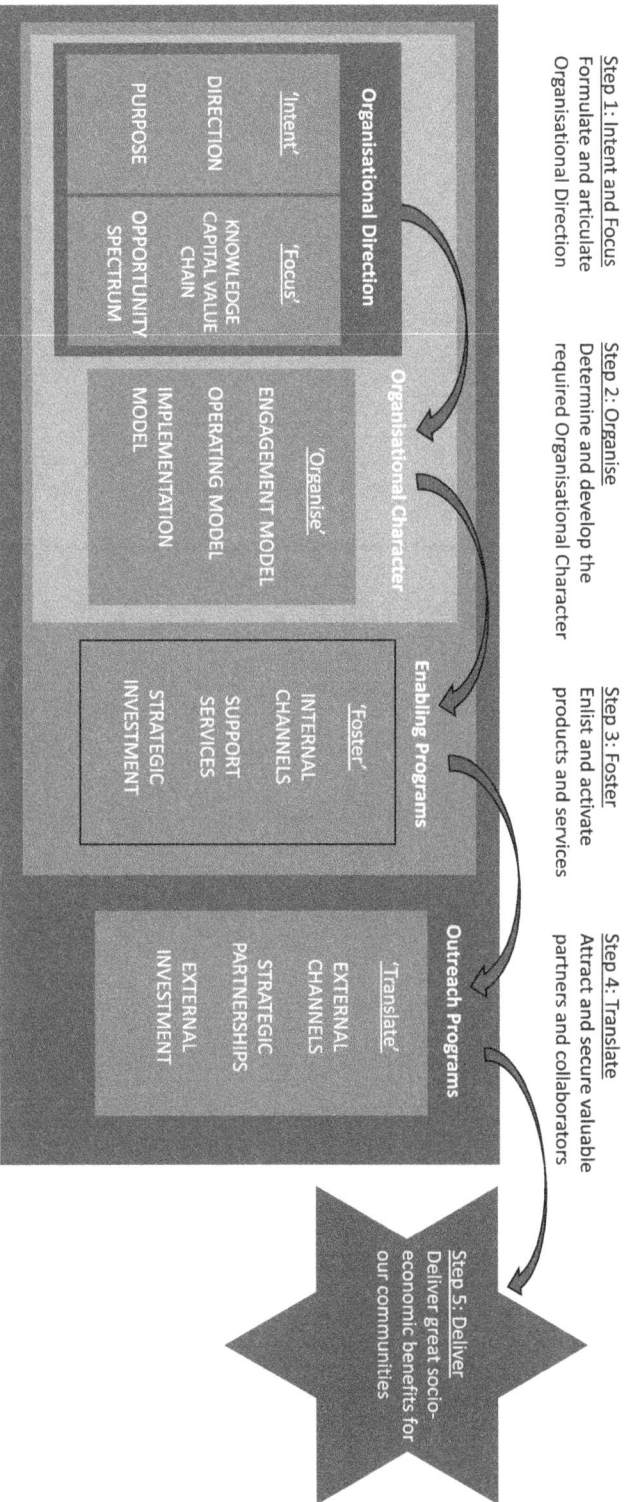

FIGURE 46: THE UNIVERSITY IMPERATIVE

Organisational Direction

'Intent'
PURPOSE
DIRECTION

'Focus'
KNOWLEDGE CAPITAL VALUE CHAIN
OPPORTUNITY SPECTRUM

Organisational Character

'Organise'
ENGAGEMENT MODEL
OPERATING MODEL
IMPLEMENTATION MODEL

Enabling Programs

'Foster'
INTERNAL CHANNELS
SUPPORT SERVICES
STRATEGIC INVESTMENT

Outreach Programs

'Translate'
EXTERNAL CHANNELS
STRATEGIC PARTNERSHIPS
EXTERNAL INVESTMENT

Step 1: Intent and Focus
Formulate and articulate
Organisational Direction

Step 2: Organise
Determine and develop the
required Organisational Character

Step 3: Foster
Enlist and activate
products and services

Step 4: Translate
Attract and secure valuable
partners and collaborators

Step 5: Deliver
Deliver great socio-
economic benefits for
our communities

ORGANISATIONAL DIRECTION

North Stars

Question 1: Whom do we serve?
Question 2: What is our ambition?
Question 3: What is our value?

Spheres of impact

Question 4: What is the societal need?
Question 5: How do we create solutions?
Question 6: How do we liberate benefits?

Knowledge-capital value chain

Question 7: What are our underlying assets?
Question 8: What are our market segments and paths-to-markets?
Question 9: What delivery mechanisms yield greatest impact?

Opportunity spectrum

Question 10: Is the consumer or organisational need well understood?
Question 11: Is the market segment strategically desirable for the university?
Question 12: Is the university's offering superior to competitors or alternatives?
Question 13: Will the university's reputation and finances be enhanced?

ORGANISATIONAL CHARACTER

Critical proficiencies

Question 14: How do we source offerings to facilitate uptake (curate)?
Question 15: How do we arrange mutually beneficial engagements (shape)?

Question 16: How do we best work with our partners and stakeholders (deliver)?

Engagement model

Question 17: What is the objective of engagement?
Question 18: What is the purpose of our engagement activities?
Question 19: What is the focus of our internal and external engagement?
Question 20: Are our engagement activities aligned with the opportunities that derive impact?
Question 21: What channels best serve our purposeful internal-engagement activities?
Question 22: What channels best serve our purposeful external-engagement activities?

Operating model

Question 23: What core processes help deliver value?
Question 24: What enabling systems will provide supporting activities and programs?
Question 25: What professional services are required to support the core processes and enabling systems?

Implementation model

Question 26: What key system-based activities are called for?
Question 27: What purposeful engagement is required?
Question 28: What purposeful activities are needed?
Question 29: What leadership and decision-making framework is appropriate?
Question 30: Which people and teams are essential?
Question 31: What strategic conversations are vital?
Question 32: What values will support coherent and aligned decision-making?

AFTERWORD

'Louis, I think this is the beginning of a beautiful friendship.'

—Rick Blaine, 'Casablanca'

Disruption, turbulence, and uncertainty are but three of the descriptions used in *The University Imperative: Delivering Socio-economic Benefits for Our World* to contextualise the 21st-century business environment. The age of globalisation has delivered us an all-encompassing climate of massive convergence.

The traditional pillars of big business are riddled with hairline fractures, stretching big business to breaking point as it struggles to come to terms with this changed landscape. No longer does big business automatically trump the small- to medium-sized enterprise. The meandering avenues through which businesses once connected with customers and suppliers have been uprooted by automation and replaced with a high-speed information highway, where a nominal fee paid instantly online secures the product or service. The physical trappings of big business no longer serve their once symbolic purpose; a well-designed home page is more valuable in impressing clients than a fully kitted-out, open-plan office space.

Digital platforms now enable anyone with an enterprising mindset to carve out their own niche business spaces, and to take ownership and control of the components of business previously placed in the hands of professionals. Technology has made readily accessible the kind of expertise associated with the roles of accountants, lawyers, advertisers, and marketing and communications and logistics professionals. The all-powerful shipping liner that once ruled the ocean is all but shipwrecked. The very idea of it still dominating the waves of commerce in the face of agile speedboats and zippy water skis borders on farcical.

For the modern university, which could be compared to big business and oceanic super-tankers, there is much food, not always palatable, for thought, as discussed in *The University Imperative: Delivering Socio-economic Benefits for Our World*. The landscape in which businesses operate today is changed utterly. The context in which business takes place is complex, complicated, and at times feels chaotic. To be successful in our business transactions today, it is crucial that the underlying characteristics of the transaction—the nature of the exchange—are reviewed.

The forthcoming book *The University Imperative: Partnering for Success* takes on this task with an in-depth exploration of the multifaceted partnership models on offer to, and being used by universities. It is these partnerships which underpin and influence the nature of exchange; it is therefore key to know all we can about the models that dictate what one organisation can both offer and procure from another. In this way, we examine the range of models in play, from the most rudimentary provision of a service to an external partner, to more sophisticated partnerships where universities engage with high-end public-private models aimed at societal benefit. We draw on examples that expand from student internships, to the funding of professorial chairs, to commercial research arrangements.

Central to this refreshed understanding of the different partnership models in play for universities are three value propositions, all of which are imperative: customer, partnership, and organisational value propositions.

In the case of customer, it is proposed that if the benefits provided do not exceed the price charged to the customer, no exchange should take place.

In the case of partnership, it is proposed that if the revenue to be recouped from the customer does not exceed the costs of providing the benefits, no exchange should take place. The inextricable link between these two value propositions is explained, along with the reasons why a university should be concerned with each as it establishes partnerships to do business.

In the case of the third value proposition, organisational value propositions, the risk to the organisation with respect to the partnership is considered, as well as the broader risk to the organisation that may materialise should the partnership be damaged. It is proposed that unless the return on investment is greater than the risk to the organisation, no exchange should take place. This exploration of value propositions will be expanded into a discussion of competitive positioning, with a practical interrogation of how the benefits-price arrangement is positioned in relation to products offered by competitors.

The exploration draws on the framework devised in *The University Imperative: Delivering Socio-economic Benefits for Our World* to drill down into examples of partnerships that reach beyond the transactional. The opportunity spectrum, for example, will be activated to identify key factors when entering a partnership, including those that differentiate your product from the wares on offer through competing platforms. The critical proficiencies will enable a clear understanding of how the value propositions operate in unison, and how the absence of the one-value proposition impacts on the other proposition and the partnership at large.

Operating landscape and contexts—already at work in this afterword—will be directly relevant to the types of partnerships identified by universities as worthwhile. They will have a bearing on the type of leadership taken into viable partnerships, and the decision-making process of university leaders. The north stars will remain a constant presence, pointing the business in productive, consistent and socially beneficial directions. The spheres-of-impact framework will be shown to keep the endgame of societal impact in sharp focus as collaboration is embarked upon.

Through this endeavour, *The University Imperative: Partnering for Success* will shape an understanding of the nature of exchange for business in the 21st century. It is an understanding that could realistically be applied to the situation of any business organisation today, but its development will maintain a university context, citing university examples. This perseverance is guided by the unflinching objective of this book, which is to reassert the humble university as an authentic and necessary means of achieving societal benefits in a much-changed world.

ABOUT THE AUTHOR

Applying his extensive experience in innovation-led, high-growth business, Nicholas Mathiou provides a pathway for universities worldwide to successfully traverse their complex and dynamic environments so they may continue to derive great societal benefits for all.

Nicholas has advised some of the largest Australian and international corporations in the creation of value through strategic acquisitions, divestments, and growth strategies. Fuelled by a desire to create innovation-based business, he leapt from the role of trusted advisor to co-found and operate a multi-million-dollar ASX-listed venture fund, eventually restructuring and positioning it for one of Australia's largest deals with an international pharmaceutical company, and then a migration to an international stock exchange listing.

Nicholas then joined an innovation and commercialisation office at a large Australian university as its Director and CEO. He utilised his wealth of commercial experience to identify and operationalise the strategic drivers relevant to the innovation-and-enterprise agenda of the university, traverse its complex organisational structures, and broaden the ways to derive great societal outcomes from the full gamut of its assets and partners. This saw a six-fold growth in revenue over a decade, and the involvement of over two-thirds of research-active staff in partnerships that derive immense societal outcomes.

Nicholas has increasingly concerned himself with both the challenges and the opportunities that our modern era presents for universities. He has applied his intimate knowledge of all aspects of the knowledge-capital value chain, from ideation to the provision of significant societal outcomes in partnership with others. His experience in successfully navigating an array of operating contexts, from all sides of the required interactions and transactions, has enabled him to present a framework that will assist universities to continually deliver abundant socio-economic benefits. It is from his unwavering belief in the important roles that universities play for society, coupled with his professional and personal perspective, that Nicholas Mathiou has put pen to paper and written *The University Imperative.*

To find out more about the author, visit:
www.au.linkedin.com/in/nicholasmathiou or
www.nicholasmathiou.com

FIGURES AND TABLES

Tables

www.ingramcontent.com/pod-product-compliance
Lightning Source LLC
Chambersburg PA
CBHW051754200326
41597CB00025B/4553